Kate Douglas Smith Wiggin

Penelope's progress; being such extracts from the commonplace book of Penelope Hamilton as relate to her experiences in Scotland

Kate Douglas Smith Wiggin

Penelope's progress; being such extracts from the commonplace book of Penelope Hamilton as relate to her experiences in Scotland

ISBN/EAN: 9783743341593

Manufactured in Europe, USA, Canada, Australia, Japa

Cover: Foto ©ninafisch / pixelio.de

Manufactured and distributed by brebook publishing software (www.brebook.com)

Kate Douglas Smith Wiggin

Penelope's progress; being such extracts from the commonplace book of Penelope Hamilton as relate to her experiences in Scotland

Penelope's Progress

BEING SUCH EXTRACTS FROM
THE COMMONPLACE BOOK
OF PENELOPE HAMILTON
AS RELATE TO HER
EXPERIENCES IN
SCOTLAND

BY

KATE DOUGLAS WIGGIN

BOSTON AND NEW YORK
HOUGHTON, MIFFLIN AND COMPANY
The Riverside Press, Cambridge
1898

CONTENTS

PART FIRST. IN TOWN

		PAGE
I.	A Triangular Alliance	1
II.	"Edina, Scotia's Darling Seat"	12
III.	A Vision in Princes Street	18
IV.	Susanna Crum couldna say	29
V.	We emulate the Jackdaw	38
VI.	Edinburgh Society, Past and Present	48
VII.	Francesca meets th' Unconquer'd Scot	60
VIII.	"What made th' Assembly shine?"	70
IX.	Omnia Presbyteria est Divisa in Partes Tres	82
X.	Mrs. M'Collop as a Sermon-Taster	93
XI.	Holyrood awakens	101
XII.	Farewell to Edinburgh	117
XIII.	The Spell of Scotland	124

PART SECOND. IN THE COUNTRY

XIV.	The Wee Theekit Hoosie in the Loaning	137
XV.	Jane Grieve and her Grievances	147
XVI.	The Path that led to Crummylowe	161
XVII.	Playing Sir Patrick Spens	168
XVIII.	Paris comes to Pettybaw	182
XIX.	Fowk o' Fife	190
XX.	A Fifeshire Tea-Party	207
XXI.	International Bickering	214
XXII.	Francesca entertains the Green-Eyed Monster	224
XXIII.	Ballad Revels at Rowardennan	234
XXIV.	Old Songs and Modern Instances	244
XXV.	A Treaty between Nations	255
XXVI.	"Scotland's burning! Look out!"	260
XXVII.	Three Magpies and a Marriage	265

PENELOPE'S PROGRESS

PART FIRST. IN TOWN

I

"Edina, Scotia's darling seat!
All hail thy palaces and towers!"

EDINBURGH, *April*, 189–.
22, Breadalbane Terrace.

WE have traveled together before, Salemina, Francesca, and I, and we know the very worst there is to know about one another. After this point has been reached, it is as if a triangular marriage had taken place, and, with the honeymoon comfortably over, we slip along in thoroughly friendly fashion. I use no warmer word than "friendly" because, in the first place, the highest tides of feeling do not visit the coast of triangular alliances; and because, in the second place, "friendly" is a word capable of putting to the blush many a more passionate and endearing one.

Every one knows of our experiences in England, for we wrote volumes of letters concerning them, the which were widely circulated among our friends at the time and read aloud under the evening lamps in the several cities of our residence.

Since then few striking changes have taken place in our history.

Salemina returned to Boston for the winter, to find, to her amazement, that for forty odd years she had been rather overestimating it.

On arriving in New York, Francesca discovered that the young lawyer whom for six months she had been advising to marry somebody "more worthy than herself" was at last about to do it. This was somewhat in the nature of a shock, for Francesca has been in the habit, ever since she was seventeen, of giving her lovers similar advice, and up to this time no one of them has ever taken it. She therefore has had the not unnatural hope, I think, of organizing at one time or another all these disappointed and faithful swains into a celibate brotherhood; and perhaps of driving by the interesting monastery with her husband and calling his attention modestly to the fact that these poor monks were filling their barren lives with deeds of piety, trying to remember their Creator with such assiduity that they might, in time, forget Her.

Her chagrin was all the keener at losing this last aspirant to her hand in that she had almost persuaded herself that she was as fond of him as she was likely to be of anybody, and that, on the whole, she had better marry him and save his life and reason.

Fortunately she had not communicated this

gleam of hope by letter, feeling, I suppose, that she would like to see for herself the light of joy breaking over his pale cheek. The scene would have been rather pretty and touching, but meantime the Worm had turned and dispatched a letter to the Majestic at the quarantine station, telling her that he had found a less reluctant bride in the person of her intimate friend Miss Rosa Van Brunt; and so Francesca's dream of duty and sacrifice was over.

Salemina says she was somewhat constrained for a week and a trifle cynical for a fortnight, but that afterwards her spirits mounted on ever ascending spirals to impossible heights, where they have since remained. It appears from all this that although she was piqued at being taken at her word, her heart was not in the least damaged. It never was one of those fragile things which have to be wrapped in cotton, and preserved from the slightest blow — Francesca's heart. It is made of excellent stout, durable material, and I often tell her with the care she takes of it, and the moderate strain to which it is subjected, it ought to be as good as new a hundred years hence.

As for me, the scene of my own love story is laid in America and England, and has naught to do with Edinburgh. It is far from finished; indeed, I hope it will be the longest serial on record, one of those charming tales that grow in interest as chapter after chapter unfolds, until at the end we feel as if we could never part with the delightful people.

I should be, at this very moment, Mrs. William Beresford, a highly respectable young matron who painted rather good pictures in her spinster days, when she was Penelope Hamilton of the great American working-class, Unlimited; but first Mrs. Beresford's dangerous illness, and then her death, have kept my dear boy a willing prisoner in Cannes, his heart sadly torn betwixt his love and duty to his mother and his desire to be with me. The separation is virtually over now, and we two, alas, have ne'er a mother or a father between us, so we shall not wait many months before beginning to comfort each other in good earnest.

Meantime Salemina and Francesca have persuaded me to join their forces, and Mr. Beresford will follow us to Scotland in a few short weeks, when we shall have established ourselves in the country.

We are overjoyed at being together again, we three women folk. As I said before, we know the worst of one another, and the future has no terrors. We have learned, for example, that:—

Francesca does not like an early morning start. Salemina refuses to arrive late anywhere. Penelope prefers to stay behind and follow next day.

Francesca scorns to travel third class. So does Salemina, but she will if urged.

Penelope hates a four-wheeler. Salemina is nervous in a hansom. Francesca prefers a Victoria.

Salemina likes a steady fire in the grate. Penelope opens a window and fans herself.

Salemina inclines to instructive and profitable expeditions. Francesca loves processions and sightseeing. Penelope abhors all of these equally.

Salemina likes history. Francesca loves fiction. Penelope adores poetry and detests facts.

Penelope likes substantial breakfasts. Francesca dislikes the sight of food in the morning.

In the matter of breakfasts, when we have leisure to assert our individual tastes, Salemina prefers tea, Francesca cocoa, and I, coffee. We can never, therefore, be served with a large comfortable pot of anything, but are confronted instead with a caravan of silver jugs, china jugs, bowls of hard and soft sugar, hot milk, cold milk, hot water, and cream, while each in her secret heart wishes that the other two were less *exigeante* in the matter of diet.

This does not sound promising, but it works perfectly well in practice by the exercise of a little flexibility.

As we left dear old Dovermarle Street and Smith's Private Hotel behind, and drove to the station to take the Flying Scotsman, we indulged in floods of reminiscence over the joys of travel we had tasted together in the past, and talked with lively anticipation of the new experiences awaiting us in the land of heather.

While Salemina went to purchase the three first-class tickets, I superintended the porters as they disposed our luggage in the van, and in so doing my eye lighted upon a third-class carriage which was, for a wonder, clean, comfortable, and vacant. Comparing it hastily with the first-class compartment being held by Francesca, I found that it differed only in having no carpet on the floor, and a smaller number of buttons in the upholstering. This was really heart-rending when the difference in fare for three persons would be at least twenty dollars. What a delightful sum to put aside for a rainy day; that is, you understand, what a delightful sum to put aside and spend on the first rainy day; for that is the way we always interpret the expression.

When Salemina returned with the tickets, she found me, as usual, bewailing our extravagance.

Francesca descended suddenly from her post, and, snatching the tickets from her duenna, exclaimed, "'I know that I can save the country, and I know no other man can!' as William Pitt said to the Duke of Devonshire. I have had enough of this argument. For six months of last year we discussed traveling third class and continued to travel first. Get into that clean, hard-seated, ill-upholstered third-class carriage immediately, both of you; save room enough for a mother with two babies, a man carrying a basket of fish, and an old woman with five pieces of hand-luggage and a dog; meanwhile I will exchange the tickets."

So saying, she disappeared rapidly among the throng of passengers, guards, porters, newspaper boys, golfers with bags of clubs, young ladies with bicycles, and old ladies with tin hat-boxes.

"What decision, what swiftness of judgment, what courage and energy!" murmured Salemina. "Isn't she wonderfully improved since that unexpected turning of the Worm?"

Francesca rejoined us just as the guard was about to lock us in, and flung herself down, quite breathless from her unusual exertion.

"Well, we are traveling third for once, and the money is saved, or at least it is ready to spend again at the first opportunity. The man did n't wish to exchange the tickets at all. He says it is never done. I told him they were bought by a very inexperienced American lady (that is you, Salemina) who knew almost nothing of the distinctions between first and third class, and naturally took the best, believing it to be none too good for a citizen of the greatest republic on the face of the earth. He said the tickets had been stamped on. I said so should I be if I returned without exchanging them. He was a very dense person, and did n't see my joke at all, but then, it is true, there were thirteen men in line behind me, with the train starting in three minutes, and there is nothing so debilitating to a naturally weak sense of humor as selling tickets behind a grating, so I am not really vexed with him. There! we are quite comfortable, pending the arrival of the babies, the dog, and the fish, and certainly no vender of periodic literature will dare approach us while we keep these books in evidence."

She had Laurence Hutton's "Literary Landmarks" and "Royal Edinburgh," by Mrs. Oliphant; I had Lord Cockburn's Memorials of his Time; and somebody had given Salemina, at the moment of leaving London, a work on "Scotia's darling seat," in three huge volumes. When all this printed matter was heaped on the top of Salemina's hold-all on the platform, the guard had asked, "Do you belong to these books, mam?"

"We may consider ourselves injured in going from London to Edinburgh in a third-class carriage in eight or ten hours, but listen to this," said Salemina, who had opened one of her large volumes at random when the train started.

"'The Edinburgh and London Stage-Coach begins on Monday, 13th October, 1712. All that desire ... let them repair to the *Coach and Horses* at the head of the Canongate every Saturday, or the *Black Swan* in Holborn every other Monday, at both of which places they may be received in a coach which performs the whole journey in thirteen days without any stoppage (if God permits) having eighty able horses. Each passenger paying £4 10s. for the whole journey, alowing each 20 lbs. weight and all above to pay 6d. per lb. The coach sets off at six in the morning' (you could never have caught it, Francesca!), 'and is performed by Henry Harrison.' And here is a 'modern improvement,' forty-two years later. In July, 1754, the 'Edinburgh Courant' advertises the stage-coach drawn by six horses, with a postilion on one of the leaders, as a 'new, genteel, two-end glass machine, hung on steel springs, exceeding light and easy, to go in ten days in summer and twelve in winter. Passengers to pay as usual. Performed (if God permits) by your dutiful servant, Hosea Eastgate. *Care is taken of small parcels according to their value.*'"

"It would have been a long, wearisome journey," said I contemplatively; "but, nevertheless, I wish we were making it in 1712 instead of a century and three quarters later."

"What would have been happening, Salemina?" asked Francesca politely, but with no real desire to know.

"The Union had been already established five years," began Salemina intelligently.

"Which Union?"

"Whose Union?"

Salemina is used to these interruptions and eruptions of illiteracy on our part. I think she rather enjoys them, as in the presence of such complete ignorance as ours her lamp of knowledge burns all the brighter.

"Anne was on the throne," she went on, with serene dignity.

"What Anne?"

"I know the Anne!" exclaimed Francesca excitedly. "She came from the Midnight Sun country, or up that way. She was very extravagant, and had something to do with Jingling Geordie in 'The Fortunes of Nigel.' It is marvelous how one's history comes back to one!"

"Quite marvelous," said Salemina dryly; "or at least the state in which it comes back is marvelous. I am not a stickler for dates, as you know, but if you could only contrive to fix a few periods in your minds, girls, just in a general way, you would not be so shamefully befogged. Your Anne of Denmark, Francesca, was the wife of James VI. of Scotland, who was James I. of England, and she died a hundred years before the Anne I mean, — the last of the Stuarts, you know. My Anne came after William and Mary, and before the Georges."

"Which William and Mary?"

"What Georges?"

But this was too much even for Salemina's

equanimity, and she retired behind her book in dignified displeasure, while Francesca and I meekly looked up the Annes in a genealogical table, and tried to decide whether "b. 1665" meant born or beheaded.

II

THE weather that greeted us on our unheralded arrival in Scotland was of the precise sort offered by Edinburgh to her unfortunate queen, when,

> "After a youth by woes o'ercast,
> After a thousand sorrows past,
> The lovely Mary once again
> Set foot upon her native plain."

John Knox records of those memorable days: "The very face of heaven did manifestlie speak what comfort was brought to this country with hir — to wit, sorrow, dolour, darkness and all impiety — for in the memorie of man never was seen a more dolorous face of the heavens than was at her arryvall . . . the myst was so thick that skairse micht onie man espy another; and the sun was not seyn to shyne two days befoir nor two days after."

We could not see Edina's famous palaces and towers because of the *haar*, that damp, chilling, drizzling, dripping fog or mist which the east wind summons from the sea; but we knew that they were there, shrouded in the heart of that opaque mysterious grayness, and that before many hours our eyes would feast upon their beauty.

Perhaps it was the weather, but I could think of nothing but poor Queen Mary! She had drifted into my imagination with the *haar*, so that I could fancy her homesick gaze across the water as she murmured, "*Adieu, ma chère France! Je ne vous verray jamais plus!*"—could fancy her saying as in Allan Cunningham's verse:—

> "The sun rises bright in France,
>   And fair sets he;
> But he hath tint the blithe blink he had
>   In my ain countree."

And then I recalled Mary's first good-night in Edinburgh: that "serenade of 500 rascals with vile fiddles and rebecks;" that singing, "in bad accord," of Protestant psalms by the wet crowd beneath the palace windows, while the fires on Arthur's Seat shot flickering gleams of welcome through the dreary fog. What a lullaby for poor Mary, half Frenchwoman and all Papist!

It is but just to remember the "indefatigable and undissuadable" John Knox's statement, "the melody lyked her weill and she willed the same to be continewed some nightis after." For my part, however, I distrust John Knox's musical feeling, and incline sympathetically to the Sieur de Brantôme's account, with its "vile fiddles" and "discordant psalms," although his judgment was doubtless a good deal depressed by what he called the *si grand brouillard* that so dampened the spirits of Mary's French retinue.

Ah well, I was obliged to remember, in order to be reasonably happy myself, that Mary had a gay heart, after all; that she was but nineteen; that, though already a widow, she did not mourn her young husband as one who could not be comforted; and that she must soon have been furnished with merrier music than the psalms, for another of the sour comments of the time is, "Our Queen weareth the dule [weeds], but she can dance daily, dule and all!"

These were my thoughts as we drove through invisible streets in the Edinburgh *haar*, turned into what proved next day to be a Crescent, and drew up to an invisible house with a visible number 22 gleaming over a door which gaslight transformed into a probability. We alighted, and though we could scarcely see the driver's outstretched hand, he was quite able to discern a half-crown, and demanded three shillings.

The noise of our cab had brought Mrs. M'Collop to the door,— good (or at least pretty good) Mrs. M'Collop, to whose apartments we had been commended by English friends who had never occupied them.

Dreary as it was without, all was comfortable within doors, and a cheery (one-and-sixpenny) fire crackled in the grate. Our private drawing-room was charmingly furnished, and so large that, notwithstanding the presence of a piano, two sofas, five small tables, cabinets, desks, and chairs, — not forgetting a dainty five-o'clock tea equipage, — we might have given a party in the remaining space.

"If this is a typical Scotch lodging I like it; and if it is Scotch hospitality to lay the cloth and make the fire before it is asked for, then I call it simply Arabian in character!" and Salemina drew off her damp gloves, and extended her hands to the blaze.

"And isn't it delightful that the bill does n't come in for a whole week?" asked Francesca. "We have only our English experiences on which to found our knowledge, and all is delicious mystery. The tea may be a present from Mrs. M'Collop, and the sugar may not be an extra; the fire may be included in the rent of the apartment, and the piano may not be taken away to-morrow to enhance the attractions of the dining-room floor." (It was Francesca, you remember, who had "warstled" with the itemized accounts at Smith's Private Hotel in London, and she who was always obliged to turn pounds, shillings, and pence into dollars and cents before she could add or subtract.)

"Come and look at the flowers in my bedroom," I called, "four great boxes full! Mr. Beresford must have ordered the carnations, because he always does; but where did the roses come from, I wonder?"

I rang the bell, and a neat white-aproned maid appeared.

"Who brought these flowers, please?"

"I couldna say, mam."

"Thank you; will you be good enough to ask Mrs. M'Collop?"

In a moment she returned with the message, "There will be a letter in the box, mam."

"It seems to me the letter should be in the box now, if it is ever to be," I thought, and I presently drew this card from among the fragrant buds:—

"Lady Baird sends these Scotch roses as a small return for the pleasure she has received from Miss Hamilton's pictures. Lady Baird will give herself the pleasure of calling to-morrow; meantime she hopes that Miss Hamilton and her party will dine with her some evening this week."

"How nice!" exclaimed Salemina.

"The celebrated Miss Hamilton's undistinguished party presents its humble compliments to Lady Baird," chanted Francesca, "and having no engagements whatever, and small hope of any, will dine with her on any and every evening she may name. Miss Hamilton's party will wear its best clothes, polish its mental jewels, and endeavor in every possible way not to injure the gifted Miss Hamilton's reputation among the Scottish nobility."

I wrote a hasty note of thanks to Lady Baird, and rang the bell.

"Can I send a message, please?" I asked the maid.

"I couldna say, mam."

"Will you be good enough to ask Mrs. M'Collop, please?"

Interval; then: —

"The Boots will tak' it at seeven o'clock, mam."

"Thank you; is Fotheringay Crescent near here?"

"I couldna say, mam."

"Thank you; what is your name, please?"

I waited in well-grounded anxiety, for I had no idea that she knew her name, or that if she had ever heard it, she could say it; but, to my surprise, she answered almost immediately, "Susanna Crum, mam!"

What a joy it is in a vexatious world, where things "gang aft agley," to find something absolutely right.

If I had devoted years to the subject, having the body of Susanna Crum before my eyes every minute of the time for inspiration, Susanna Crum is what I should have named that maid. Not a vowel could be added, not a consonant omitted. I said so when first I saw her, and weeks of intimate acquaintance only deepened my reverence for the parental genius that had so described her to the world.

III

WHEN we awoke next morning the sun had forgotten itself and was shining in at Mrs. M'Collop's back windows.

We should have arisen at once to burn sacrifices and offer oblations, but we had seen the sun frequently in America, and had no idea (poor fools!) that it was anything to be grateful for, so we accepted it, almost without comment, as one of the perennial providences of life.

When I speak of Edinburgh sunshine I do not mean, of course, any such burning, whole-souled, ardent warmth of beam as one finds in countries where they make a specialty of climate. It is, generally speaking, a half-hearted, uncertain ray, as pale and as transitory as a martyr's smile; but its faintest gleam, or its most puerile attempt to gleam, is admired and recorded by its well-disciplined constituency. Not only that, but at the first timid blink of the sun the true Scotsman remarks smilingly, "I think now we shall be having settled weather!" It is a pathetic optimism, beautiful but quite groundless, and leads one to believe in the story that when Father Noah refused to take Sandy into the ark, he sat down philosophically outside, saying, with a glance at the clouds, "Aweel! the day's jist aboot the ord'nar', an' I wouldna won'er if we saw the sun afore nicht!"

.But what loyal son of Edina cares for these transatlantic gibes, and where is the dweller within her royal gates who fails to succumb to the sombre beauty of that old gray town of the North? "Gray! why, it is gray, or gray and gold, or gray and gold and blue, or gray and gold and blue and green, or gray and gold and blue and green and purple, according as the heaven pleases and you choose your ground! But take it when it is most sombrely gray, where is another such gray city?"

So says one of her lovers, and so the great army of lovers would say, had they the same gift of language; for

> "Even thus, methinks, a city reared should be, . . .
> Yea, an imperial city that might hold
> Five times a hundred noble towns in fee. . . .
> Thus should her towers be raised; with vicinage
> Of clear bold hills, that curve her very streets,
> As if to indicate, 'mid choicest seats
> Of Art, abiding Nature's majesty."

We ate a hasty breakfast that first morning, and prepared to go out for a walk into the great unknown, perhaps the most pleasurable sensation in the world. Francesca was ready first, and, having mentioned the fact several times ostentatiously, she went into the drawing-room to wait and read "The Scotsman." When we went thither a few minutes later we found that she had disappeared.

"She is below, of course," said Salemina. "She fancies that we shall feel more ashamed at our tardiness if we find her sitting on the hall bench in silent martyrdom."

There was no one in the hall, however, save Susanna, who inquired if we would see the cook before going out.

"We have no time now, Susanna," I remarked. "We are anxious to have a walk before the weather changes if possible, but we shall be out for luncheon and in for dinner, and Mrs. M'Collop may give us anything she pleases. Do you know where Miss Francesca is?"

"I couldna s—"

"Certainly, of course you couldn't; but I wonder if Mrs. M'Collop saw her?"

Mrs. M'Collop appeared from the basement, and vouchsafed the information that she had seen "the young leddy rinnin' after the regiment."

"Running after the regiment!" repeated Salemina automatically. "What a reversal of the laws of nature! Why, in Berlin, it was always the regiment that used to run after her!"

We learned in what direction the soldiers had gone, and pursuing the same path found the young lady on the corner of a street near by. She was quite unabashed. "You don't know what you have missed!" she said excitedly. "Let us get into this tram, and possibly we can head them off somewhere. They may be going into battle, and if so my heart's blood is at their service. It is one of those experiences that come only once in a lifetime. There were pipes and there were kilts! (I did n't suppose they ever really wore them outside of the theatre!) When you have seen the kilts swinging, Salemina, you will never be the same woman afterwards! You never expected to see the Olympian gods walking, did you? Perhaps you thought they always sat on practicable rocks and made stiff gestures from the elbow, as they do in the Wagner operas? Well, these gods walked, if you can call the inspired gait a walk! If there is a single spinster left in Scotland, it is because none of these ever asked her to marry him. Ah, how grateful I ought to be that I am free to say 'yes,' if a kilt ever asks me to be his! Poor Penelope, yoked to your commonplace trousered Beresford! (I wish the tram would go faster!) You must capture one of them, by fair means or foul, Penelope, and Salemina and I will hold him down while you paint him, — there they are, they are there somewhere, don't you hear them?"

There they were indeed, filing down the grassy slopes of the Gardens, swinging across one of the stone bridges, and winding up the Castle Hill to the Esplanade like a long, glittering snake; the streamers of their Highland bonnets waving, their arms glistening in the sun, and the bagpipes playing "The March of the Cameron Men." The pipers themselves were mercifully hidden from us on that first occasion, and it was well, for we could never have borne another feather's weight of ecstasy.

It was in Princes Street that we had alighted, — named thus for the prince who afterwards became George IV. — and I hope he was, and is, properly grateful. It ought never to be called a street, this most magnificent of terraces, and the world has cause to bless that interdict of the Court of Sessions in 1774, which prevented the Gradgrinds of the day from erecting buildings along its south side, — a sordid scheme that would have been the very superfluity of naughtiness.

It was an envious Glasgow body who said grudgingly, as he came out of Waverley Station, and gazed along its splendid length for the first time, "*Weel, wi' a' their haverin', it's but half a street, onyway!*" — which always reminded me of the Western farmer who came from his native plains to the beautiful Berkshire hills. "I've always heard o' this scenery," he said. "Blamed if I can find any scenery; but if there was, nobody could see it, there's so much high ground in the way!"

To think that not so much more than a hundred years ago Princes Street was naught but a straight country road, the "Lang Dykes" and the "Lang Gait," as it was called.

We looked down over the grassy chasm that separates the New from the Old Town; looked our first on Arthur's Seat, that crouching lion of a mountain; saw the Corstorphine hills, and Calton Heights, and Salisbury Crags, and finally that stupendous bluff of rock that culminates so majestically in Edinburgh Castle. There is something else which, like Susanna Crum's name, is absolutely and ideally right! Stevenson calls it one of the most satisfactory crags in nature — a Bass rock upon dry land, rooted in a garden, shaken by passing trains, carrying a crown of battlements and turrets, and describing its warlike shadow over the liveliest and brightest thoroughfare of the new town. It dominates the whole countryside from water and land. The men who would have the courage to build such a castle in such a spot are all dead; all dead, and the world is infinitely more comfortable without them. They are all gone, and no more like unto them will ever be born, and we can most of us count upon dying safely in our beds, of diseases bred of modern civilization. But I am glad that those old barbarians, those rudimentary creatures working their way up into the divine likeness, when they were not hanging, drawing, quartering, torturing, and chopping their neighbors, and using their heads in conventional patterns on the tops of gate-posts, did devote their leisure intervals to rearing fortresses like this. Edinburgh Castle could not be conceived, much less built, nowadays, when all our energy is consumed in bettering the condition of the "submerged tenth"! What did they care about the "masses," that "regal race that is now no more," when they were hewing those blocks of rugged rock and piling them against the sky-line on the top of that great stone mountain! It amuses me to think how much more picturesque they left the world, and how much better we shall leave it; though if an artist were requested to distribute individual awards to different generations, you could never persuade him to give first prizes to the centuries that produced steam laundries, trolleys, X rays, and sanitary plumbing.

What did they reck of Peace Congresses and bloodless arbitrations when they lighted the beacon-fires, flaming out to the gudeman and his sons ploughing or sowing in the Lang Dykes the news that their "ancient enemies of England had crossed the Tweed"!

I am the most peaceful person in the world, but the Castle was too much for my imagination. I was mounted and off and away from the first moment I gazed upon its embattled towers, heard the pipers in the distance, and saw the Black Watch swinging up the green steeps where the huge fortress "holds its state." The modern world had vanished, and my steed was galloping, galloping, galloping back into the place-of-the-things-that-are-past, traversing centuries at every leap.

"To arms! Let every banner in Scotland float defiance to the breeze!" (So I heard my new-born imaginary spirit say to my real one.) "Yes, and let the Deacon Convener unfurl the sacred Blue Blanket, under which every liege burgher of the kingdom is bound to answer summons! The bale-fires are gleaming, giving alarm to Hume, Haddington, Dunbar, Dalkeith, and Eggerhope. Rise, Stirling, Fife, and the North! All Scotland will be under arms in two hours. One bale-fire: the English are in motion! Two: they are advancing! Four in a row: they are of great strength! All men in arms west of Edinburgh muster there! All eastward, at Haddington! And every Englishman caught in Scotland is lawfully the prisoner of whoever takes him!" (What am I saying? I love Englishmen, but the spell is upon me!) "Come on, Macduff!" (The only suitable and familiar challenge my warlike tenant can summon at the moment.) "I am the son of a Gael! My dagger is in my belt, and with the guid broadsword at my side I can with one blow cut a man in twain! My bow is cut from the wood of the yews of Glenure; the shaft is from the wood of Lochetive, the feathers from the great golden eagles of Lochtreigside! My arrowhead was made by the smiths of the race of Macphedran! Come on, Macduff!"

And now a shopkeeper has filled his window with royal Stuart tartans, and I am instantly a Jacobite.

> "The Highland clans wi' sword in hand,
>   Frae John o' Groat's to Airly,
> Hae to a man declar'd to stand
>   Or fa' wi' Royal Charlie.
> Come through the heather, around him gather,
> Come Ronald, come Donald, come a' thegither,
> And crown your rightfu', lawfu' king,
>   For wha'll be king but Charlie?"

It is the eve of the battle of Prestonpans. Is it not under the Rock of Dunsappie on yonder Arthur's Seat that our Highland army will encamp to-night? At dusk the prince will hold a council of his chiefs and nobles (I am a chief and a noble), and at daybreak we shall march through the old hedgerows and woods of Duddingston, pipes playing and colors flying, bonnie Charlie at the head, his claymore drawn and the scabbard flung away! (I mean awa'!)

> "Then here's a health to Charlie's cause,
>   And be 't complete an' early;
> His very name my heart's blood warms
>   To arms for Royal Charlie!

> "Come through the heather, around him gather,
> Come Ronald, come Donald, come a' thegither,
> And crown your rightfu', lawfu' king,
>   For wha'll be king but Charlie?"

I hope that those in authority will never attempt

to convene a peace congress in Edinburgh, lest the influence of the Castle be too strong for the delegates. They could not resist it nor turn their backs upon it, since, unlike other ancient fortresses, it is but a stone's throw from the front windows of all the hotels. They might mean never so well, but they would end by buying dirk hat-pins and claymore brooches for their wives, their daughters would all run after the kilted regiment and marry as many of the pipers as asked them, and before night they would all be shouting with the noble Fitz-Eustace,

> " Where's the coward who would not dare
> To fight for such a land ? "

While I was rhapsodizing, Salemina and Francesca were shopping in the Arcade, buying some of the cairn-gorms, and Tam O'Shanter purses, and models of Burns's cottage, and copies of " Marmion " in plaided covers, and thistle beltbuckles, and bluebell penwipers, with which we afterwards inundated our native land. When my warlike mood had passed, I sat down upon the steps of the Scott monument and watched the passers-by in a sort of waking dream. I suppose they were the usual professors and doctors and ministers who are wont to walk up and down the Edinburgh streets, with a sprinkling of lairds and leddies of high degree and a few Americans looking at the shop windows to choose their clantartans ; but for me they did not exist. In their places stalked the ghosts of kings and queens and knights and nobles: Columba, Abbot of Iona; Queen Margaret and Malcolm — she the sweetest saint in all the throng; King David riding towards Drumsheugh forest on Holy Rood-day, with his horns and hounds and huntsmen following close behind; Anne of Denmark and Jingling Geordie; Mary Stuart in all her girlish beauty, with the four Maries in her train; and lurking behind, Bothwell, "that ower sune stepfaither," and the murdered Rizzio and Darnley; John Knox, in his black Geneva cloak; Bonnie Prince Charlie and Flora Macdonald; lovely Annabella Drummond; Robert the Bruce; George Heriot with a banner bearing on it the words " I distribute chearfully;" James I. carrying The King's Quair; Oliver Cromwell; and a long line of heroes, martyrs, humble saints, and princely knaves.

Behind them, regardless of precedence, came the Ploughman Poet and the Ettrick Shepherd, Boswell and Dr. Johnson, Dr. John Brown and Thomas Carlyle, Lady Nairne and Drummond of Hawthornden, Allan Ramsay and Sir Walter; and is it not a proof of the Wizard's magic art, that side by side with the wraiths of these real people walked, or seemed to walk, the Fair Maid of Perth, Jeanie Deans, Meg Merrilies, Guy Mannering, Ellen, Marmion, and a host of others so sweetly familiar and so humanly dear that the very street-laddies could have named and greeted them as they passed by?

IV

LIFE at Mrs. M'Collop's apartments in 22, Breadalbane Terrace is about as simple, comfortable, dignified, and delightful as it well can be.

Mrs. M'Collop herself is neat, thrifty, precise, tolerably genial, and "verra releegious."

Her partner, who is also the cook, is a person introduced to us as Miss Diggity. We afterwards learned that this is spelled Dalgety, but it is not considered good form, in Scotland, to pronounce the names of persons and places as they are written. When, therefore, I allude to the cook, which will be as seldom as possible, I shall speak of her as Miss Diggity-Dalgety, so that I shall be presenting her correctly both to the eye and to the ear, and giving her at the same time a hyphenated name, a thing which is a secret object of aspiration in Great Britain.

In selecting our own letters and parcels from the common stock on the hall table, I perceive that most of our fellow lodgers are hyphenated ladies, whose visiting-cards diffuse the intelligence that in their single persons two ancient families and fortunes are united. On the ground floor are the Misses Hepburn-Sciennes (pronounced Hebburn-Sheens); on the floor above us are Miss Colquhoun (Cohoon) and her cousin Miss Cockburn-Sinclair (Coburn-Sinkler). As soon as the Hepburn-Sciennes depart, Mrs. M'Collop expects Mrs. Menzies of Kilconquhar, of whom we shall speak as Mrs. Mingess of Kinyukkar. There is not a man in the house; even the Boots is a girl, so that 22, Breadalbane Terrace is as truly a *castra puellarum* as was ever the Castle of Edinburgh with its maiden princesses in the olden time.

We talked with Miss Diggity-Dalgety on the evening of our first day at Mrs. M'Collop's, when she came up to know our commands. As Francesca and Salemina were both in the room, I determined to be as Scotch as possible, for it is Salemina's proud boast that she is taken for a native of every country she visits.

"We shall not be entertaining at present, Miss Diggity," I said, "so you can give us just the ordinary dishes, — no doubt you are accustomed to them: scones, baps or bannocks with marmalade, finnan-haddie or kippered herrings for breakfast; tea, — of course we never touch coffee in the morning" (here Francesca started with surprise); "porridge, and we like them well boiled, please" (I hope she noted the plural pronoun; Salemina did, and blanched with envy); "minced collops for luncheon, or a nice little black-faced chop; Scotch broth, peas brose or cockyleekie soup, at dinner, and haggis now and then, with a cold shape for dessert. That is about the sort of thing we are accustomed to, — just plain Scotch living."

I was impressing Miss Diggity-Dalgety, — I could see that clearly; but Francesca spoiled the effect by inquiring, maliciously, if we could sometimes have a howtowdy wi' drappit eggs, or her favorite dish, wee grumphie wi' neeps.

Here Salemina was obliged to poke the fire in order to conceal her smiles, and the cook probably suspected that Francesca found howtowdy in the Scotch glossary; but we amused each other vastly, and that is our principal object in life.

Miss Diggity-Dalgety's forbears must have been exposed to foreign influences, for she interlards her culinary conversation with French terms, and we have discovered that this is quite common. A "jigget" of mutton is of course a *gigot*, and we have identified an "ashet" as an *assiette*. The "petticoat tails" she requested me to buy at the confectioner's were somewhat more puzzling, but when they were finally purchased by Susanna Crum they appeared to be ordinary little cakes; perhaps, therefore, *petits gastels*, since gastel is an old form of *gâteau*, as was *bel* for *beau*. Susanna, on her part, speaks of the wardrobe in my bedroom as an "awmry." It certainly contains no weapons, so cannot be an armory, and we conjecture that her word must be a corruption of *armoire*.

"That was a remarkable touch about the black-faced chop," laughed Salemina, when Miss Diggity-Dalgety had retired; "not that I believe they ever say it."

"I am sure they must," I asserted stoutly, "for I passed a flesher's on my way home, and saw a sign with 'Prime Black-faced Mutton' printed on it. I also saw 'Fed Veal,' but I forgot to ask the cook for it."

"We ought really to have kept house in Edinburgh," observed Francesca, looking up from "The Scotsman." "One can get a 'self-contained residential flat' for twenty pounds a month. We are such an enthusiastic trio that a self-contained flat would be everything to us; and if it were not fully furnished, here is a firm that wishes to sell a 'composite bed' for six pounds, and a 'gent's stuffed easy' for five. Added to these inducements there is somebody who advertises that parties who intend 'displenishing' at the Whit Term would do well to consult him, as he makes a specialty of second-handed furniture and 'cyclealities.' What are 'cyclealities,' Susanna?" (She had just come in with coals.)

"I couldna say, mam."

"Thank you; no, you need not ask Mrs. M'Collop; it is of no consequence."

Susanna Crum is a most estimable young woman, clean, respectful, willing, capable, and methodical, but as a Bureau of Information she is painfully inadequate. Barring this single limitation she seems to be a treasure-house of all good practical qualities; and being thus clad and panoplied in virtue, why should she be so timid and self-distrustful?

She wears an expression which can mean only one of two things: either she has heard of the national tomahawk and is afraid of violence on our part, or else her mother was frightened before she was born. This applies in general to her walk and voice and manner, but is it fear that prompts her eternal "I couldna say," or is it perchance Scotch caution and prudence? Is she afraid of projecting her personality too indecently far? Is it the influence of the "catecheesm" on her early youth? Is it the indirect effect of heresy trials on her imagination? Does she remember the thumb-screw of former generations? At all events, she will neither affirm nor deny, and I am putting her to all sorts of tests, hoping to discover finally whether she is an accident, an exaggeration, or a type.

Salemina thinks that our American accent may confuse her. Of course she means Francesca's and mine, for she has none; although we have tempered ours so much for the sake of the natives, that we can scarcely understand each other any more. As for Susanna's own accent, she comes from the heart of Aberdeenshire, and her intonation is beyond my power to reproduce.

We naturally wish to identify all the national dishes; so, "Is this cockle soup, Susanna?" I ask her, as she passes me the plate at dinner.

"I couldna say."

"This vegetable is new to me, Susanna; is it perhaps sea-kail?"

"I canna say, mam."

Then finally, in despair, as she handed me a boiled potato one day, I fixed my searching Yankee brown eyes on her blue-Presbyterian, non-committal ones and asked, "What is this vegetable, Susanna?"

In an instant she withdrew herself, her soul, her ego, so utterly that I felt myself gazing at an inscrutable stone image, as she replied, "I couldna say, mam."

This was too much! Her mother may have been frightened, very badly frightened, but this was more than I could endure without protest. The plain boiled potato is practically universal. It is not only common to all temperate climates, but it has permeated all classes of society. I am confident that the plain boiled potato has been one of the chief constituents in the building up of that frame in which Susanna Crum conceals her opinions and emotions. I remarked, therefore, as an apparent afterthought, "Why, it is a potato, is it not, Susanna?"

What do you think she replied, when thus hunted into a corner, pushed against a wall, driven to the very confines of her personal and national liberty? She subjected the potato to a second careful scrutiny, and answered, "I wouldna say it's no!"

Now there is no inherited physical terror in this. It is the concentrated essence of intelligent reserve, caution, and obstinacy; it is a conscious intellectual hedging; it is a dogged and determined attempt to build up barriers of defense between the questioner and the questionee: it must be, therefore, the offspring of the catechism and the heresy trial.

Once again, after establishing an equally obvious fact, I succeeded in wringing from her the reluctant admission, "It depends," but she was so shattered by the bulk and force of this outgo, so fearful that in some way she had imperiled her life or reputation, so anxious concerning the effect that her unwilling testimony might have upon unborn generations, that she was of no real service the rest of the day.

I wish that the Lord Advocate, or some modern counterpart of Braxfield, the hanging judge, would summon Susanna Crum as a witness in an important case. He would need his longest plummet to sound the depths of her consciousness.

I have had no legal experience, but I can imagine the scene.

"Is the prisoner your father, Susanna Crum?"

"I couldna say, my lord."

"You have not understood the question, Susanna. Is the prisoner your father?"

"I couldna say, my lord."

"Come, come, my girl! you must answer the questions put you by the court. You have been an inmate of the prisoner's household since your earliest consciousness. He provided you with food, lodging, and clothing during your infancy and early youth. You have seen him on annual visits to your home, and watched him as he performed the usual parental functions for your younger brothers and sisters. I therefore repeat, is the prisoner your father, Susanna Crum?"

"I wouldna say he's no, my lord."

"This is really beyond credence! What do you conceive to be the idea involved in the word 'father,' Susanna Crum?"

"It depends, my lord."

And this, a few hundred years earlier, would have been the natural and effective moment for the thumb-screws.

I do not wish to be understood as defending these uncomfortable appliances. They would never have been needed to elicit information from me, for I should have spent my nights inventing matter to confess in the daytime. I feel sure that I should have poured out such floods of confessions and retractations that if all Scotland had been one listening ear it could not have heard my tale. I am only wondering if, in the extracting of testimony from the common mind, the thumb-screw might not have been more necessary with some nations than with others.

V

INVITATIONS had been pouring in upon us since the delivery of our letters of introduction, and it was now the evening of our début in Edinburgh society. Francesca had volunteered to perform the task of leaving cards, ordering a private victoria for the purpose, and arraying herself in purple and fine linen.

"Much depends upon the first impression," she had said. "Miss Hamilton's 'party' may not be gifted, but it is well dressed. My hope is that some of our future hostesses will be looking from the second-story front windows. If they are, I can assure them in advance that I shall be a national advertisement."

It is needless to remark that as it began to rain heavily as she was leaving the house, she was obliged to send back the open carriage, and order, to save time, one of the public cabs from the stand in the Terrace.

"Would you mind having the lamiter, being first in line?" asked Susanna of Salemina, who had transmitted the command.

When Salemina fails to understand anything, the world is kept in complete ignorance, — least of all would she stoop to ask a humble maid servant to translate the vernacular of the country; so she replied affably, " Certainly, Susanna, that is the kind we always prefer. I suppose it is covered?"

Francesca did not notice, until her coachman alighted to deliver the first letter and cards, that he had one club foot and one wooden leg; it was then that the full significance of " lamiter " came to her. He was covered, however, as Salemina had supposed, and the occurrence gave us a precious opportunity of chaffing that dungeon of learning. He was tolerably alert and vigorous, too, although he certainly did not impart elegance to a vehicle, and he knew every street in the court end of Edinburgh, and every close and wynd in the Old Town. On this our first meeting with him, he faltered only when Francesca asked him last of all to drive to " Kildonan House, Helmsdale;" supposing, not unnaturally, that it was as well known an address as Morningside House, Tipperlinn, whence she had just come. The lamiter had never heard of Kildonan House nor of Helmsdale, and he had driven in the streets of Auld Reekie for thirty years. None of the drivers whom he consulted could supply any information; Susanna Crum couldna say that she had ever heard of it, nor could Mrs. M'Collop nor Miss Diggity-Dalgety. It was reserved for Lady Baird to explain that Helmsdale was two hundred and eighty miles north, and that Kildonan House was ten miles from the Helmsdale railway station, so that the poor lamiter would have had a weary drive even had he known the way. The friends who had given us letters to Mr. and Mrs. Jameson-Inglis (Jimmyson-Ingals) must have expected us either to visit John o' Groat's on the northern border, and drop in on Kildonan House *en route*, or to send our note of introduction by post and await an invitation to pass the summer. At all events, the anecdote proved very pleasing to our Edinburgh acquaintances. I hardly know whether, if they should visit America, they would enjoy tales of their own stupidity as hugely as they did the tales of ours, but they really were very appreciative in this particular, and it is but justice to ourselves to say that we gave them every opportunity for enjoyment.

But I must go back to our first grand dinner in Scotland. We were dressed at quarter past seven, when, in looking at the invitation again, we discovered that the dinner-hour was eight o'clock, not seven-thirty. Susanna did not happen to know the exact or approximate distance to Fotheringay Crescent, but the maiden Boots affirmed that it was only two minutes' drive, so we sat down in front of the fire to chat.

It was Lady Baird's birthday feast to which we had been bidden, and we had done our best to honor the occasion. We had prepared a large bouquet tied with the Maclean tartan (Lady

Baird is a Maclean), and had printed in gold letters on one of the ribbons, "Another for Hector," the battle-cry of the clan. We each wore a sprig of holly, because it is the badge of the family, while I added a girdle and shoulder-knot of tartan velvet to my pale green gown, and borrowed Francesca's emerald necklace, persuading her that she was too young to wear such jewels in the old country.

Francesca was miserably envious that she had not thought of tartans first. "You may consider yourself 'gey an' fine,' all covered over with Scotch plaid, but I would n't be so 'kenspeckle' for worlds!" she said, using expressions borrowed from Mrs. M'Collop; "and as for disguising your nationality, do not flatter yourself that you look like anything but an American. I forgot to tell you the conversation I overheard in the tram this morning, between a mother and daughter, who were talking about us, I dare say. 'Have they any proper frocks for so large a party, Bella?' asked the mother.

"'I thought I explained in the beginning, mamma, that they are Americans.'

"'Still, you know they are only traveling,—just passing through, as it were; they may not be familiar with our customs, and we do want our party to be a smart one.'

"'Wait until you see them, mamma, and you will probably feel like hiding your diminished head! It is my belief that if an American lady takes a half-hour journey in a tram she carries full evening dress and a diamond necklace, in case anything should happen on the way. I am not in the least nervous about their appearance. I only hope that they will not be too exuberant; American girls are so frightfully vivacious and informal, I always feel as if I were being taken by the throat!'"

"A picturesque, though rather vigorous expression; however, it does no harm to be perfectly dressed," said Salemina consciously, putting a steel embroidered slipper on the fender and settling the holly in the silver folds of her gown; "then when they discover that we are all well bred, and that one of us is intelligent, it will be the more credit to the country that gave us birth."

"Of course it is impossible to tell what country did give *you* birth," retorted Francesca, "but that will only be to your advantage — away from home!"

Francesca is inflexibly, almost aggressively American, but Salemina is a citizen of the world. If the United States should be involved in a war, I am confident that Salemina would be in front with the other Gatling guns, for in that case a principle would be at stake; but in all lesser matters she is extremely unprejudiced. She prefers German music, Italian climate, French dressmakers, English tailors, Japanese manners, and American — American something, — I have forgotten just what; it is either the ice-cream soda or the form of government, — I can't remember which.

"I wonder why they named it 'Fotheringay' Crescent," mused Francesca. "Some association with Mary Stuart, of course. Poor, poor, pretty lady! A free queen only six years, and think of the number of beds she slept in, and the number of trees she planted; we have already seen, I am afraid to say how many. When did she govern, when did she scheme, above all when did she flirt, with all this racing and chasing over the country? Mrs. M'Collop calls Anne of Denmark a 'sad scattercash' and Mary an 'awfu' gadabout,' and I am inclined to agree with her. By the way, when she was making my bed this morning, she told me that her mother claimed descent from the Stewarts of Appin, whoever they may be. She apologized for Queen Mary's defects as if she were a distant family connection. If so, then the famous Stuart charm has been lost somewhere, for Mrs. M'Collop certainly possesses no alluring curves of temperament."

"I am going to select some distinguished ancestors this very minute, before I go to my first Edinburgh dinner," said I decidedly. "It seems hard that ancestors should have everything to do with settling our nationality and our position in life, and we not have a word to say. How nice it would be to select one's own after one had arrived at years of discretion, or to adopt different ones according to the country one chanced to be visiting! I am going to do it; it is unusual, but there must be a pioneer in every good movement. Let me think: do help me, Salemina! I am a Hamilton to begin with; I might be descended from the logical Sir William himself, and thus become the idol of the university set!"

"He died only about thirty years ago, and you would have to be his daughter: that would never do," said Salemina. "Why don't you take Thomas Hamilton, Earl of Melrose and Haddington? He was Secretary of State, King's Advocate, Lord President of the Court of Sessions, and all sorts of fine things. He was the one King James used to call 'Tam o' the Cowgate.'"

"Perfectly delightful! I don't care so much about his other titles, but 'Tam o' the Cowgate' is irresistible. I will take him. He was my — what was he?"

"He was at least your great-great-great-great-grandfather; that is a safe distance. Then there's that famous Jenny Geddes, who flung her fauldstule at the Dean in St. Giles's, — she was a Hamilton, too, if you fancy her!"

"Yes, I'll take her with pleasure," I responded thankfully. "Of course I don't know why she flung the stool, — it may have been very reprehensible; but there is always good stuff in stoolflingers; it's the sort of spirit one likes to inherit in diluted form. Now whom will you take?"

"I haven't even a peg on which to hang a Scottish ancestor," said Salemina disconsolately.

"Oh, nonsense! think harder. Anybody will do as a starting-point; only you must be honorable and really show relationship, as I did with Jenny and Tam."

"My aunt Mary-Emma married a Lindsay," ventured Salemina hesitatingly.

"That will do," I answered delightedly.

> "'The Gordons gay in English blude
> They wat their hose and shoon;
> The Lindsays flew like fire aboot
> Till a' the fray was dune.'

You can play that you are one of the famous 'licht Lindsays,' and you can look up the particular ancestor in your big book. Now, Francesca, it's your turn!"

"I am American to the backbone," she declared, with insufferable dignity. "I do not desire any foreign ancestors."

"Francesca!" I expostulated. "Do you mean to tell me that you can dine with a lineal descendant of Sir Fitzroy Donald Maclean, Baronet, of Duart and Morven, and not make any effort to trace your genealogy back further than your parents?"

"If you goad me to desperation," she answered, "I will wear an American flag in my hair, declare that my father is a Red Indian, or a pork-packer, and talk about the superiority of our checking system and hotels all the evening. I don't want to go, anyway. It is sure to be stiff and ceremonious, and the man who takes me in will ask me the population of Chicago and the amount of wheat we exported last year, — he always does."

"I can't see why he should," said I. "I am sure you don't look as if you knew."

"My looks have thus far proved no protection," she replied sadly. "Salemina is so flexible, and you are so dramatic, that you enter into all these experiences with zest. You already more than half believe in that Tam o' the Cowgate story. But there'll be nothing for me in Edinburgh society; it will be all clergymen" —

"Ministers," interjected Salemina.

—"all ministers and professors. My Redfern gown will be unappreciated, and my Worth evening frocks worse than wasted!"

"There are a few thousand medical students," I said encouragingly, "and all the young advocates, and a sprinkling of military men, — they know Worth frocks."

"And," continued Salemina bitingly, "there will always be, even in an intellectual city like Edinburgh, a few men who continue to escape all the developing influences about them, and remain commonplace, conventional manikins, devoted to dancing and flirting. Never fear, they will find you!"

This sounds harsh, but nobody minds Salemina, least of all Francesca, who well knows she is the apple of that spinster's eye. But at this moment Susanna opens the door (timorously, as if there might be a panther behind it) and announces the cab (in the same tone in which she would announce the beast); we pick up our draperies, and are whirled off by the lamiter to dine with the Scottish nobility.

VI

It was the Princess Dashkoff who said, in the latter part of the eighteenth century, that of all the societies of men of talent she had met with in her travels, Edinburgh's was the first in point of abilities.

One might make the same remark to-day, perhaps, and not depart widely from the truth. One does not find, however, as many noted names as are associated with the annals of the Cape and Poker Clubs or the Crochallan Fencibles, those famous groups of famous men who met for relaxation (and intoxication, I should think) at the old Isle of Man Arms or in Dawney's Tavern in the Anchor Close. These groups included such shining lights as Robert Fergusson the poet, and Adam Ferguson the historian and philosopher, Gavin Wilson, Sir Henry Raeburn, David Hume, Erskine, Lords Newton, Gillies, Monboddo, Hailes, Kames, Henry Mackenzie, and the Ploughman Poet himself, who has kept alive the memory of the Crochallans in many a jovial verse like that in which he describes Smellie, the eccentric philosopher and printer : —

> " Shrewd Willie Smellie to Crochallan came,
> The old cocked hat, the grey surtout the same,
> His bristling beard just rising in its might ;
> 'T was four long nights and days to shaving night ; "

or in the characteristic picture of William Dunbar, a wit of the time, and the merriest of the Fencibles: —

> "As I cam by Crochallan
>   I cannily keekit ben;
> Rattlin', roarin' Willie
>   Was sitting at yon boord en';
> Sitting at yon boord en',
>   And amang guid companie!
> Rattlin', roarin' Willie,
>   Ye 're welcome hame to me!"

or in the verses on Creech, Burns's publisher, who left Edinburgh for a time in 1789. The "Willies," by the way, seem to be especially inspiring to the Scottish balladists.

> "Oh, Willie was a witty wight,
>   And had o' things an unco slight!
> Auld Reekie aye he keepit tight
>   And trig and braw;
> But now they 'll busk her like a fright —
>   Willie 's awa'!"

I think perhaps the gatherings of the present time are neither quite as gay nor quite as brilliant as those of Burns's day, when

> "Willie brewed a peck o' maut,
>   An' Rob an' Allan cam to pree;"

but the ideal standard of those meetings seems to be voiced in the lines: —

> "Wha last beside his chair shall fa',
>   He is the king amang us three!"

As they sit in their chairs nowadays to the very end of the feast, there is doubtless joined with modern sobriety a *soupçon* of modern dullness and discretion.

To an American the great charm of Edinburgh is its leisurely atmosphere: "not the leisure of a village arising from the deficiency of ideas and motives, but the leisure of a city reposing grandly on tradition and history; which has done its work, and does not require to weave its own clothing, to dig its own coals, or smelt its own iron."

We were reminded of this more than once, and it never failed to depress us properly. If one had ever lived in Pittsburg, Fall River, or Kansas City, I should think it would be almost impossible to maintain self-respect in a place like Edinburgh, where the citizens "are released from the vulgarizing dominion of the hour." Whenever one of Auld Reekie's great men took this tone with me, I always felt as though I were the germ in a half-hatched egg, and he were an aged and lordly cock gazing at me pityingly through my shell. He, lucky creature, had lived through all the struggles which I was to undergo; he, indeed, was released from "the vulgarizing dominion of the hour;" but I, poor thing, must grow and grow, and keep pecking at my shell, in order to achieve existence.

Sydney Smith says in one of his letters, "Never

shall I forget the happy days passed there [in Edinburgh], amidst odious smells, barbarous sounds, bad suppers, excellent hearts, and the most enlightened and cultivated understandings." His only criticism of the conversation of that day (1797–1802) concerned itself with the prevalence of that form of Scotch humor which was called *wut*, and with the disputations and dialectics. We were more fortunate than Sydney Smith, because Edinburgh has outgrown its odious smells, barbarous sounds, and bad suppers, and, wonderful to relate, has kept its excellent hearts and its enlightened and cultivated understandings. As for mingled *wut* and dialectics, where can one find a better foundation for dinner-table conversation?

The hospitable board itself presents no striking differences from our own, save the customs of serving sweets in soup-plates with dessert-spoons, of a smaller number of forks on parade, of the invariable fish-knife at each plate, of the prevalent "savory" and "cold shape," and the unusual grace and skill with which the hostess carves. Even at very large dinners one occasionally sees a lady of high degree severing the joints of chickens and birds most daintily, while her lord looks on in happy idleness, thinking, perhaps, how greatly times have changed for the better since the ages of strife and bloodshed, when Scottish nobles

"Carved at the meal with gloves of steel,
And drank their wine through helmets barred."

The Scotch butler is not in the least like an English one. No man could be as respectable as he looks, not even an elder of the kirk, whom he resembles closely. He hands your plate as if it were a contribution-box, and in his moments of ease, when he stands behind the "maister," I am always expecting him to pronounce a benediction. The English butler, when he wishes to avoid the appearance of listening to the conversation, gazes with level eye into vacancy; the Scotch butler looks distinctly heavenward, as if he were brooding on the principle of coördinate jurisdiction with mutual subordination. It would be impossible for me to deny the key of the wine-cellar to a being so steeped in sanctity, but it has been done, I am told, in certain rare and isolated cases.

As for toilets, the men dress like all other men (alas, and alas, that we should say it, for we were continually hoping for a kilt!), though there seems to be no survival of the finical Lord Napier's spirit. Perhaps you remember that Lord and Lady Napier arrived at Castlemilk in Lanarkshire with the intention of staying a week, but announced next morning that a circumstance had occurred which rendered it indispensable to return without delay to their seat in Selkirkshire. This was the only explanation given, but it was afterwards discovered that Lord Napier's valet had committed the grievous mistake of packing up a set of neck-cloths which did not correspond *in point of date* with the shirts they accompanied!

The ladies of the "smart set" in Edinburgh wear French fripperies and *chiffons*, as do their sisters everywhere, but the other women of society dress a trifle more staidly than their cousins in London, Paris, or New York. The sobriety of taste and severity of style that characterize Scotswomen may be due, like Susanna Crum's dubieties, to the *haar*, to the shorter catechism, or perhaps in some degree to the presence of three branches of the Presbyterian church among them; the society that bears in its bosom three separate and antagonistic kinds of Presbyterianism at the same time must have its chilly moments.

In Lord Cockburn's time the "dames of high and aristocratic breed" must have been sufficiently awake to feminine frivolities to be both gorgeously and extravagantly arrayed. I do not know in all literature a more delicious and lifelike word-portrait than Lord Cockburn gives of Mrs. Rochead, the Lady of Inverleith, in the Memorials. It is quite worthy to hang beside a Raeburn canvas; one can scarce say more.

"Except Mrs. Siddons in some of her displays of magnificent royalty, nobody could sit down like the Lady of Inverleith. She would sail like a ship from Tarshish, gorgeous in velvet or rustling silk, done up in all the accompaniments of fans, ear-rings and finger-rings, falling sleeves, scent-bottle, embroidered bag, hoop, and train; managing all this seemingly heavy rigging with as much ease as a full-blown swan does its plumage. She would take possession of the centre of a large sofa, and at the same moment, without the slightest visible exertion, cover the whole of it with her bravery, the graceful folds seeming to lay themselves over it, like summer waves. The descent from her carriage, too, where she sat like a nautilus in its shell, was a display which no one in these days could accomplish or even fancy. The mulberry-colored coach, apparently not too large for what it contained, though she alone was in it; the handsome, jolly coachman and his splendid hammer-cloth loaded with lace; the two respectful liveried footmen, one on each side of the richly carpeted step, — these were lost sight of amidst the slow majesty with which the Lady of Inverleith came down and touched the earth."

My right-hand neighbor at Lady Baird's dinner was surprised at my quoting Lord Cockburn. One's attendant squires here always seem surprised when one knows anything; but they are always delighted, too, so that the amazement is less trying. True, I had read the Memorials only the week before, and had never heard of them previous to that time; but that detail, according to my theories, makes no real difference. The woman who knows how and when to "read up," who reads because she wants to be in sympathy with a new environment; the woman who has wit and perspective enough to be stimulated by novel conditions and kindled by fresh influences, who is susceptible to the vibrations of other people's history, is safe to be fairly intelligent and extremely agreeable, if only she is sufficiently modest. I think my neighbor found me thoroughly delightful after he discovered my point of view. He was an earl; and it always takes an earl a certain length of time to understand me. I scarcely know why, for I certainly should not think it courteous to interpose any real barriers between the nobility and that portion of the "masses" represented in my humble person.

It seemed to me at first that the earl did not apply himself to the study of my national peculiarities with much assiduity, but wasted considerable time in gazing at Francesca, who was opposite. She is certainly very handsome, and I never saw her lovelier than at that dinner; her eyes were like stars, and her cheeks and lips a splendid crimson, for she was quarreling with her attendant cavalier about the relative merits of Scotland and America, and they apparently ceased to speak to each other after the salad.

When the earl had sufficiently piqued me by

his devotion to his dinner and his glances at Francesca, I began a systematic attempt to achieve his (transient) subjugation. Of course I am ardently attached to Willie Beresford and prefer him to any earl in Britain, but one's self-respect demands something in the way of food. I could see Salemina at the far end of the table radiant with success, the W. S. at her side bending ever and anon to catch the (artificial) pearls of thought that dropped from her lips. "Miss Hamilton appears simple" (I thought I heard her say); "but in reality she is as deep as the Currie Brig!" Now where did she get that allusion? And again, when the W. S. asked her whither she was going when she left Edinburgh, "I hardly know," she replied pensively. "I am waiting for the shade of Montrose to direct me, as the Viscount Dundee said to your Duke of Gordon." The entranced Scotsman little knew that she had perfected this style of conversation by long experience with the Q. C.'s of England. Talk about my being as deep as the Currie Brig (whatever it may be); Salemina is deeper than the Atlantic Ocean! I shall take pains to inform her Writer to the Signet, after dinner, that she eats sugar on her porridge every morning; that will show him her nationality conclusively.

The earl took the greatest interest in my new ancestors, and approved thoroughly of my choice.

He thinks I must have been named for Lady Penelope Belhaven, who lived in Leven Lodge, one of the country villas of the Earls of Leven, from whom he himself is descended. "Does that make us relatives?" I asked. "Relatives, most assuredly," he replied, "but not too near to destroy the charm of friendship."

He thought it a great deal nicer to select one's own forbears than to allow them all the responsibility, and said it would save a world of trouble if the method could be universally adopted. He added that he should be glad to part with a good many of his, but doubted whether I would accept them, as they were "rather a scratch lot." (I use his own language, which I thought delightfully easy for a belted earl.) He was charmed with the story of Francesca and the lāmiter, and offered to drive me to Kildonan House, Helmsdale, on the first fine day. I told him he was quite safe in making the proposition, for we had already had the fine day, and we understood that the climate had exhausted itself and retired for the season.

The gentleman on my right, a distinguished Dean of the Thistle, gave me a few moments' discomfort by telling me that the old custom of "rounds" of toasts still prevailed at Lady Baird's on formal occasions, and that before the ladies retired every one would be called upon for appropriate "sentiments."

"What sort of sentiments?" I inquired, quite overcome with terror.

"Oh, epigrammatic sentences expressive of moral feelings or virtues," replied my neighbor easily. "They are not quite as formal and hackneyed now as they were in the olden time, when some of the favorite toasts were 'May the pleasure of the evening bear the reflections of the morning!' 'May the friends of our youth be the companions of our old age!' 'May the honest heart never feel distress!' 'May the hand of charity wipe the eye of sorrow!'"

"I can never do it in the world!" I ejaculated. "Oh, one ought never, never to leave one's own country! A light-minded and cynical English gentleman told me that I should frequently be called upon to read hymns and recite verses of Scripture at family dinners in Edinburgh and I hope I am always prepared to do that; but nobody warned me that I should have to evolve epigrammatic sentiments on the spur of the moment."

My confusion was so evident that the good dean relented and confessed that he was imposing upon my ignorance. He made me laugh heartily at the story of a poor dominie at Arndilly. He was called upon in his turn, at a large party, and having nothing to aid him in an exercise to which he was new save the example of his predecessors, lifted his glass after much writhing and groaning and gave, "The reflection of the moon in the cawm bosom of the lake!"

At this moment Lady Baird glanced at me, and we all rose to go into the drawing-room; but on the way from my chair to the door, whither the earl escorted me, he said gallantly, "I suppose the men in your country do not take champagne at dinner? I cannot fancy their craving it when dining beside an American woman!"

That was charming, though he did pay my country a compliment at my expense. One likes, of course, to have the type recognized as fine; at the same time his remark would have been more flattering if it had been less sweeping.

When I remember that he offered me his ancestors, asked me to drive two hundred and eighty miles, and likened me to champagne, I feel that, with my heart already occupied and my hand promised, I could hardly have accomplished more in the course of a single dinner-hour.

VII

FRANCESCA'S experiences were not so fortunate; indeed, I have never seen her more out of sorts than she was during our long chat over the fire, after our return to Breadalbane Terrace.

"How did you get on with your delightful minister?" inquired Salemina of the young lady, as she flung her unoffending wrap over the back of a chair. "He was quite the handsomest man in the room; who is he?"

"He is the Reverend Ronald Macdonald, and the most disagreeable, condescending, ill-tempered prig I ever met!"

"Why, Francesca!" I exclaimed. "Lady Baird speaks of him as her favorite nephew, and says he is full of charm."

"He is just as full of charm as he was when I met him," returned the girl nonchalantly; "that is, he parted with none of it this evening. He was incorrigibly stiff and rude, and oh! so Scotch! I believe if one punctured him with a hat-pin, oatmeal would fly into the air!"

"Doubtless you acquainted him, early in the evening, with the immeasurable advantages of our sleeping-car system, the superiority of our fast-running elevators, and the height of our buildings?" observed Salemina.

"I mentioned them," Francesca answered evasively.

"You naturally inveighed against the Scotch climate?"

"Oh, I alluded to it; but only when he said that our hot summers must be insufferable."

"I suppose you repeated the remark you made at luncheon, that the ladies you had seen in Princes Street were excessively plain?"

"Yes, I did!" she replied hotly; "but that was because he said that American girls generally looked bloodless and frail. He asked if it were really true that they ate chalk and slate pencils. Was n't that unendurable? I answered that those were the chief solid articles of food, but that after their complexions were established, so to speak, their parents often allowed them pickles and native claret to vary the diet."

"What did he say to that?" I asked.

"Oh, he said, 'Quite so, quite so;' that was his invariable response to all my witticisms. Then when I told him casually that the shops looked very small and dark and stuffy here, and that there were not as many tartans and plaids in the windows as we had expected, he remarked that as to the latter point, the American season had not opened yet! Presently he asserted that no royal city in Europe could boast ten centuries of such glorious and stirring history as Edinburgh. I said it did not appear to be stirring much at present, and that everything in Scotland seemed a little slow to an American; that he could have no idea of push or enterprise until he visited a city like Chicago. He retorted that, happily, Edinburgh was peculiarly free from the taint of the ledger and the counting-house; that it was Weimar without a Goethe, Boston without its twang!"

"Incredible!" cried Salemina, deeply wounded in her local pride. "He never could have said 'twang' unless you had tried him beyond measure!"

"I dare say I did; he is easily tried," returned Francesca. "I asked him, sarcastically, if he had ever been in Boston. 'No,' he said, 'it is not necessary to *go* there! And while we are discussing these matters,' he went on, 'how is your American dyspepsia these days,—have you decided what is the cause of it?'

"'Yes, we have,' said I, as quick as a flash; 'we have always taken in more foreigners than we could assimilate!' I wanted to tell him that one Scotsman of his type would upset the national digestion anywhere, but I restrained myself."

"I am glad you did restrain yourself—once," exclaimed Salemina. "What a tactful person the Reverend Ronald must be, if you have reported him faithfully! Why did n't you give him up, and turn to your other neighbor?"

"I did, as soon as I could with courtesy; but the man on my left was the type that always haunts me at dinners; if the hostess has n't one on her visiting-list, she imports one for the occasion. He asked me at once of what material the Brooklyn Bridge is made. I told him I really did n't know. Why should I? I seldom go over it. Then he asked me whether it was a suspension bridge or a cantilever. Of course I did n't know; I am not an engineer."

"You are so tactlessly, needlessly candid," I expostulated. "Why did n't you say boldly that the Brooklyn Bridge is a wooden cantilever, with gutta-percha braces? He did n't know, or he would n't have asked you. He could n't find out until he reached home, and you would never have seen him again; and if you had, and he had taunted you, you could have laughed vivaciously and said you were chaffing. That is my method, and it is the only way to preserve life in a foreign country. Even my earl, who did not thirst for information (fortunately), asked me the population of the Yellowstone Park, and I simply told him three hundred thousand, at a venture."

"That would never have satisfied my neighbor," said Francesca. "Finding me in such a lamentable state of ignorance, he explained the principle of his own stupid Forth Bridge to me. When I said I understood perfectly, just to get into shallower water, where we would n't need any bridge, the Reverend Ronald joined in the conversation, and asked me to repeat the explanation to him. Naturally I could n't, and he knew that I could n't when he asked me, so the bridge man (I don't know his name, and don't care to know it) drew a diagram of the national idol on his dinner-card and gave a dull and elaborate lecture upon it. Here is the card, and now that three hours have intervened I cannot tell which way to turn the drawing so as to make the bridge right side up; if there is anything puzzling in the world, it is these architectural plans and diagrams. I am going to pin it to the wall and ask the Reverend Ronald which way it goes."

"Do you mean that he will call upon us?" we cried in concert.

"He asked if he might come and continue our 'stimulating' conversation, and as Lady Baird was standing by I could hardly say no. I am sure of one thing: that before I finish with him I will widen his horizon so that he will be able to see something beside Scotland and his little insignificant Fifeshire parish! I told him our country parishes in America were ten times as large as his. He said he had heard that they covered a good deal of territory, and that the ministers' salaries were sometimes paid in pork and potatoes. That shows you the style of his retorts!"

"I really cannot decide which of you was the

more disagreeable," said Salemina; "if he calls, I shall not remain in the room."

"I would n't gratify him by staying out," retorted Francesca. "He is extremely good for the circulation; I think I was never so warm in my life as when I talked with him; as physical exercise he is equal to bicycling. The bridge man is coming to call, too. I gave him a diagram of Breadalbane Terrace, and a plan of the hall and staircase, on my dinner-card. He was distinctly ungrateful; in fact, he remarked that he had been born in this very house, but would not trust himself to find his way upstairs with my plan as a guide. He also said the American vocabulary was vastly amusing, so picturesque, unstudied, and fresh."

"That was nice, surely," I interpolated.

"You know perfectly well that it was an insult."

"Francesca is very like the young man," laughed Salemina, "who, whenever he engaged in controversy, seemed to take off his flesh and sit in his nerves."

"I'm not supersensitive," replied Francesca, "but when one's vocabulary is called picturesque by a Britisher, one always knows he is thinking of cowboys and broncos. However, I shifted the weight into the other scale by answering, 'Thank you. And your phraseology is just as unusual to us.' 'Indeed?' he said with some surprise. 'I supposed our method of expression very sedate and uneventful.' 'Not at all,' I returned, 'when you say, as you did a moment ago, that you never eat potato to your fish.' 'But I do not,' he urged obtusely. 'Very likely,' I argued, 'but the fact is not of so much importance as the preposition. Now I eat potato *with* my fish.' 'You make a mistake,' he said, and we both laughed in spite of ourselves, while he murmured, 'eating potato *with* fish, — how extraordinary.' Well, the bridge man may not add perceptibly to the gayety of the nations, but he is better than the Reverend Ronald. I forgot to say that when I chanced to be speaking of doughnuts, that 'unconquer'd Scot' asked me if a doughnut resembled a peanut! Can you conceive such ignorance?"

"I think you were not only aggressively American, but painfully provincial," said Salemina, with some warmth. "Why in the world should you drag doughnuts into a dinner-table conversation in Edinburgh? Why not select topics of universal interest?"

"Like the Currie Brig or the shade of Montrose," I murmured slyly.

"To one who has ever eaten a doughnut, the subject is of transcendent interest; and as for one who has not — well, he should be made to feel his limitations," replied Francesca, with a yawn. "Come, let us forget our troubles in sleep; it is after midnight."

About half an hour later she came to my bedside, her dark hair hanging over her white gown, her eyes still bright.

"Penelope," she said softly, "I did not dare tell Salemina, and I should not confess it to you save that I am afraid Lady Baird will complain of me; but I was dreadfully rude to the Reverend Ronald! I could n't help it; he roused my worst passions. It all began with his saying he thought international marriages presented even more difficulties to the imagination than the other kind. *I* had n't said anything about marriages nor thought anything about marriages of any sort, but I told him *instantly* I considered that every international marriage involved two national suicides. He said that he should n't have put it quite so forcibly, but that he had n't given much thought to the subject. I said that *I* had, and I thought we had gone on long enough filling the coffers of the British nobility with American gold."

"*Frances!*" I interrupted. "Don't tell me that you made that vulgar, cheap newspaper assertion!"

"I did," she replied stoutly, "and at the moment I only wished I could make it stronger. If there had been anything cheaper or more vulgar, I should have said it, but of course there is n't. Then he remarked that the British nobility merited and needed all the support it could get in these hard times, and asked if we had not cherished some intention in the States, lately, of bestowing it in greenbacks instead of gold! I threw all manners to the winds after that and told him that there were no husbands in the world like American men, and that foreigners never seemed to háve any proper consideration for women. Now, were my remarks any worse than his, after all, and what shall I do about it, anyway?"

"You should go to bed first," I murmured sleepily; "and if you ever have an opportunity to make amends, which I doubt, you should devote yourself to showing the Reverend Ronald the breadth of your own horizon instead of trying so hard to broaden his. As you are extremely pretty, you may possibly succeed; man is human, and I dare say in a month you will be advising him to love somebody more worthy than yourself. (He could easily do it!) Now don't kiss me again, for I am displeased with you; I hate international bickering!"

"So do I," agreed Francesca virtuously, as she plaited her hair, "and there is no spectacle so abhorrent to every sense as a narrow-minded man who cannot see anything outside of his own country. But he is awfully good-looking, — I will say that for him; and if you don't explain me to Lady Baird, I will write to Mr. Beresford about the earl. There was no bickering there; it was looking at you two that made us think of international marriages."

"It must have suggested to you that speech about filling the coffers of the British nobility," I replied sarcastically, "inasmuch as the earl has twenty thousand pounds a year, probably, and I could barely buy two gold hairpins to pin on the coronet. There, do go away and leave me in peace!"

"Good-night again, then," she said, as she rose reluctantly from the foot of the bed. "I doubt if I can sleep for thinking what a pity it is that such an egotistic, bumptious, pugnacious, prejudiced, insular, bigoted person should be so handsome! And who wants to marry him, anyway, that he should be so distressed about international alliances? One would think that all female America was sighing to lead him to the altar!"

VIII

Two or three days ago we noted an unusual though subdued air of excitement at 22, Breadalbane Terrace, where for a week we had been the sole lodgers. Mrs. Menzies, whom we call Mingess, has returned to Kilconquhar, which she calls Kinyukkar; Miss Cockburn-Sinclair has purchased her wedding outfit and gone back to Inverness, where she will be greeted as Coburn-Sinkler; the Hepburn-Sciennes will be leaving to-morrow, just as we have learned to pronounce their names; and the sound of the scrubbing-brush is heard in the land. In corners where all was clean and spotless before, Mrs. M'Collop is digging with the broom, and the maiden Boots is following her with a damp cloth. The stair carpets are hanging on lines in the back garden, and Susanna, with her cap rakishly on one side, is always to be seen polishing the stair rods. Whenever we traverse the halls we are obliged to leap over pails of suds, and Miss Diggity-Dalgety has given us two dinners which bore a curious resemblance to washing-day repasts in suburban America.

"Is it spring house-cleaning?" I ask Mistress M'Collop.

"Na, na," she replies hurriedly; "it's the meenisters."

On the 19th of May we are a maiden castle no longer. Black coats and hats ring at the bell, and pass in and out of the different apartments. The hall table is sprinkled with letters, visiting-cards, and programmes which seem to have had the alphabet shaken out upon them, for they bear the names of professors, doctors, reverends, and very reverends, and fairly bristle with A. M.'s, M. A.'s, A. B.'s, D. D.'s, and LL. D.'s. The voice of family prayer is lifted up from the dining-room floor, and Paraphrases and hymns float down the stairs from above. Their Graces the Lord High Commissioner and the Marchioness of Heatherdale will arrive to-day at Holyrood Palace, there to reside during the sittings of the General Assembly of the Church of Scotland, and to-morrow the Royal Standard will be hoisted at Edinburgh Castle from reveille to retreat. His Grace will hold a levee at eleven. Directly His Grace leaves the palace after the levee, the guard of honor will proceed by the Canongate to receive him on his arrival at St. Giles' Church, and will then proceed to Assembly Hall to receive him on his arrival there. The Sixth Inniskilling Dragoons and the First Battalion Royal Scots will be in attendance, and there will be unicorns, carricks, pursuivants, heralds, mace-bearers, ushers, and pages, together with the Purse-bearer, and the Lyon King-of-Arms, and the national anthem, and the royal salute; for the palace has awakened and is "mimicking its past."

"Should the weather be wet the troops will be cloaked at the discretion of the commanding officers." They print this instruction as a matter of form, and of course every man has his mackintosh ready. The only hope lies in the fact that this is a national function, and "Queen's weather" is a possibility. The one personage for whom the Scottish climate will occasionally relax is Her Majesty Queen Victoria, who for sixty years has exerted a benign influence on British skies and at least secured sunshine on great parade days. Such women are all too few!

In this wise enters His Grace the Lord High Commissioner to open the General Assembly of the Church of Scotland; and on the same day there arrives by the railway (but traveling first class) the Moderator of the Church of Scotland, Free, to convene its separate Supreme Courts in Edinburgh. He will have no Union Jacks, Royal Standards, Dragoons, bands, or pipers; he will bear his own purse and stay at a hotel; but when the final procession of all comes, he will probably march beside His Grace the Lord High Commissioner, and they will talk together, not of dead-and-gone kingdoms, but of the one at hand, where there are no more divisions in the ranks, and where all the soldiers are simply "king's men," marching to victory under the inspiration of a common watchword.

It is a matter of regret to us that the U. P.'s, the third branch of Scottish Presbyterianism, could not be holding an Assembly during this same week, so that we might the more easily decide in which flock we really belong. 22, Breadalbane Terrace now represents all shades of religious opinion within the bounds of Presbyterianism. We have an Elder, a Professor of Biblical Criticism, a Majesty's Chaplain, and even an ex-Moderator under our roof, and they are equally divided between the Free and the Established bodies.

Mrs. M'Collop herself is a pillar of the Free Kirk, but she has no prejudice in lodgers, and says so long as she "mak's her rent she doesna care aboot their releegious principles." Miss Diggity-Dalgety is the sole representative of United Presbyterianism in the household, and she is somewhat gloomy in Assembly time. To belong to a dissenting body, and yet to cook early and late for the purpose of fattening one's religious rivals, is doubtless trying to the temper; and then she asserts that "meenisters are aye tume [empty]."

"You must put away your Scottish ballads and histories now, Salemina, and keep your Concordance and your umbrella constantly at hand."

This I said as we stood on George IV. Bridge and saw the ministers glooming down from the Mound in a dense Assembly fog. As the presence of any considerable number of priests on an ocean steamer is supposed to bring rough weather, so the addition of a few hundred parsons to the population of Edinburgh is believed to induce rain, — or perhaps I should say, more rain.

Of course, when one is in perfect bodily health one can more readily resist the infection of disease. Similarly if Scottish skies were not ready and longing to pour out rain, were not ignobly weak in holding it back, they would not be so susceptible to the depressing influences of visiting ministers. This is Francesca's theory as stated to the Reverend Ronald, who was holding an umbrella over her ungrateful head at the time; and she went on to boast of a convention she once attended in San Francisco, where twenty-six thousand Christian Endeavorers were unable to dim the California sunshine, though they stayed ten days.

"Our first duty, both to ourselves and to the community," I continued to Salemina, "is to learn how there can be three distinct kinds of proper Presbyterianism. Perhaps it would be a graceful act on our part if we should each espouse a different kind; then there would be no feeling among our Edinburgh friends. And again, what is this 'union' of which we hear murmurs? Is it religious or political? Is it an echo of the 1707 Union you explained to us last week, or is it a new one? What is Disestablishment? What is Disruption? Are they the same thing? What is the Sustentation Fund? What was the Non-Intrusion Party? What was the Dundas Despotism? What is the argument at present going on about taking the Shorter Catechism out of the schools? What is the Shorter Catechism, anyway, — or at least, what have they left out of the Longer Catechism to make it shorter, — and is the length of the Catechism one of the points of difference? Then when we have looked up Chalmers and Candlish, we can ask the ex-Moderator and the Professor of Biblical Criticism to tea; separately, of course, lest there should be ecclesiastical quarrels."

Salemina and Francesca both incline to the Established Church, I lean instinctively toward the Free; but that does not mean that we have any knowledge of the differences that separate them. Salemina is a conservative in all things; she loves law, order, historic associations, old customs; and so when there is a regularly established national church, — or, for that matter, a regularly established anything, — she gravitates to it by the law of her being. Francesca's religious convictions, when she is away from her own minister and native land, are inclined to be flexible. The church that enters Edinburgh with a marquis and a marchioness representing the Crown, the church that opens its Assembly with splendid processions and dignified pageants, the church that dispenses generous hospitality from Holyrood Palace, — above all, the church that escorts its Lord High Commissioner from place to place with bands and pipers, — that is the church to which she pledges her constant presence and enthusiastic support.

As for me, I believe I am a born protestant, or "come-outer," as they used to call dissenters in the early days of New England. I have not yet had time to study the question, but as I lack all knowledge of the other two branches of Presbyterianism, I am enabled to say unhesitatingly that I belong to the Free Kirk. To begin with, the very word "free" has a fascination for the citizen of a republic; and then my theological training was begun this morning by a gifted young minister of Edinburgh whom we call the Friar, because the first time we saw him in his gown and bands (the little spot of sheer whiteness beneath the chin, that lends such added spirituality to a spiritual face) we fancied that he looked like some pale brother of the Church in the olden time. His pallor, in a land of rosy redness and milky whiteness; his smooth, fair hair, which in the light from the stained-glass window above the pulpit looked reddish gold;

the Southern heat of passionate conviction that colored his slow Northern speech; the remoteness of his personality; the weariness of his deep-set eyes, that bespoke such fastings and vigils as he probably never practiced, — all this led to our choice of the name.

As we walked toward St. Andrew's Church and Tanfield Hall, where he insisted on taking me to get the "proper historical background," he told me about the great Disruption movement. He was extremely eloquent, — so eloquent that the image of Willie Beresford tottered continually on its throne, and I found not the slightest difficulty in giving an unswerving allegiance to the principles presented by such an orator.

We went first to St. Andrew's, where the General Assembly met in 1843, and where the famous exodus of the Free Protesting Church took place, — one of the most important events in the modern history of the United Kingdom.

The movement was promoted by the great Dr. Chalmers and his party, mainly to abolish the patronage of livings, then in the hands of certain heritors or patrons, who might appoint any minister they wished, without consulting the congregation. Needless to say, as a free-born American citizen, and never having had a heritor in the family, my blood easily boiled at the recital of such tyranny. In 1834 the Church had passed a law of its own, it seems, ordaining that no presentee to a parish should be admitted, if opposed by the majority of the male communicants. That would have been well enough could the State have been made to agree, though I should have gone further, personally, and allowed the female communicants to have some voice in the matter.

The Friar took me into a particularly chilly historic corner, and, leaning against a damp stone pillar, painted the scene in St. Andrew's when the Assembly met in the presence of a great body of spectators, while a vast throng gathered without, breathlessly awaiting the result. No one believed that any large number of ministers would relinquish livings and stipends and cast their bread upon the waters for what many thought a "fantastic principle." Yet when the Moderator left his place, after reading a formal protest signed by one hundred and twenty ministers and seventy-two elders, he was followed first by Dr. Chalmers, and then by four hundred and seventy men, who marched in a body to Tanfield Hall, where they formed themselves into the General Assembly of the Free Church of Scotland. When Lord Jeffrey was told of it an hour later, he exclaimed, "Thank God for Scotland! There is not another country on earth where such a deed could be done!" And the Friar reminded me proudly of Macaulay's saying that the Scots had made sacrifices for the sake of religious opinion for which there was no parallel in the annals of England. On the next Sunday after these remarkable scenes in Edinburgh there were heart-breaking farewells, so the Friar said, in many village parishes, when the minister, in dismissing his congregation, told them that he had ceased to belong to the Established Church and would neither preach nor pray in that pulpit again; that he had joined the Free Protesting Church of Scotland, and, God willing, would speak the next Sabbath morning at the manse door to as many as cared to follow him. "What affecting leave-takings there must have been!" the Friar exclaimed. "When my grandfather left his church that May morning, only fifteen members remained behind, and he could hear the more courageous say to the timid ones, 'Tak' your Bible an' come awa' mon!' Was not all this a splendid testimony to the power of principle and the sacred demands of conscience?" I said "Yea" most heartily, for the spirit of Jenny Geddes stirred within me that morning, and under the spell of the Friar's kindling eye and eloquent voice I positively gloried in the valiant achievements of the Free Church. It would always be easier for a woman to say "Yea" than "Nay" to the Friar. When he left me in Breadalbane Terrace I was at heart a member of his congregation in good (and irregular) standing, ready to teach in his Sunday-school, sing in his choir, visit his aged and sick poor, and especially to stand between him and a too admiring feminine constituency.

When I entered the drawing-room, I found that Salemina had just enjoyed an hour's conversation with the ex-Moderator of the opposite church wing.

"Oh, my dear," she sighed, "you have missed such a treat! You have no conception of these Scottish ministers of the Establishment,—such culture, such courtliness of manner, such scholarship, such spirituality, such wise benignity of opinion! I asked the doctor to explain the Disruption movement to me, and he was most interesting and lucid, and most affecting, too, when he described the misunderstandings and misconceptions that the Church suffered in those terrible days of 1843, when its very life-blood, as well as its integrity and unity, was threatened by the foes in its own household; when breaches of faith and trust occurred on all sides, and dissents and disloyalties shook it to its very foundation! You see, Penelope, I have never fully understood the disagreements about heritors and livings and state control before, but here is the whole matter in a nut-sh—"

"My dear Salemina," I interposed, with dignity, "you will pardon me, I am sure, when I tell you that any discussion on this point would be intensely painful to me, as I now belong to the Free Kirk."

"Where have you been this morning?" she asked, with a piercing glance.

"To St. Andrew's and Tanfield Hall."

"With whom?"

"With the Friar."

"I see! Happy the missionary to whom you incline your ear, *first!*"—which I thought rather inconsistent of Salemina, as she had been converted by precisely the same methods and in precisely the same length of time as had I, the only difference being in the ages of our respective missionaries, one being about five and thirty, the other five and sixty. Even this is to my credit after all, for if one can be persuaded so quickly and fully by a young and comparatively inexperienced man, it shows that one must be extremely susceptible to spiritual influences or — something.

IX

Religion in Edinburgh is a theory, a convention, a fashion (both humble and aristocratic), a sensation, an intellectual conviction, an emotion, a dissipation, a sweet habit of the blood; in fact, it is, it seems to me, every sort of thing it can be to the human spirit.

When we had finished our church toilettes, and came into the drawing-room, on the first Sunday morning, I remember that we found Francesca at the window.

"There is a battle, murder, or sudden death going on in the square below," she said. "I am going to ask Susanna to ask Mrs. M'Collop what it means. Never have I seen such a crowd moving peacefully, with no excitement or confusion, in one direction. Where can the people be going? Do you suppose it is a fire? Why, I believe . . . it cannot be possible . . . yes, they certainly are disappearing in that big church on the corner; and millions, simply millions and trillions, are coming in the other direction, — toward St. Knox's."

Impressive as was this morning church-going, a still greater surprise awaited us at seven o'clock in the evening, when the crowd blocked the streets on two sides of a church near Breadalbane Terrace; and though it was quite ten minutes before service when we entered, Salemina and I only secured the last two seats in the aisle, and Francesca was obliged to sit on the steps of the pulpit or seek a sermon elsewhere.

It amused me greatly to see Francesca sitting on pulpit steps, her Paris gown and smart toque in close juxtaposition to the rusty bonnet and bombazine dress of a respectable elderly tradeswoman. The church officer entered first, bearing the great Bible and hymn-book, which he reverently placed on the pulpit cushions; and close behind him, to our entire astonishment, came the Reverend Ronald Macdonald, evidently exchanging with the regular minister of the parish, whom we had come especially to hear. I pitied Francesca's confusion and embarrassment, but I was too far from her to offer an exchange of seats, and through the long service she sat there at the feet of her foe, so near that she could have touched the hem of his gown as he knelt devoutly for his first silent prayer.

Perhaps she was thinking of her last interview with him, when she descanted at length on that superfluity of naughtiness and Biblical pedantry which, she asserted, made Scottish ministers preach from out-of-the-way texts.

"I've never been able to find my place in the Bible since I arrived," she complained to Salemina, when she was quite sure that Mr. Macdonald was listening to her; and this he generally was, in my opinion, no matter who chanced to be talking. "What with their skipping and hopping about from Haggai to Philemon, Habakkuk to Jude, and Micah to Titus, in their readings, and then settling on seventh Nahum, sixth Zephaniah or second Calathumpians for the sermon, I do nothing but search the Scriptures in the Edinburgh churches, — search, search, search, until some Christian by my side or in the pew behind me notices my hapless plight, and hands me a Bible opened at the text. Last Sunday it was Obadiah first, fifteenth, 'For the day of the Lord is near upon all the heathen.' It chanced to be a returned missionary who was preaching on that occasion; but the Bible is full of heathen, and why need he have chosen a text from Obadiah, poor little Obadiah one page long, slipped in between Amos and Jonah, where nobody but an elder could find him?" If Francesca had not seen with wicked delight the Reverend Ronald's expression of anxiety, she would never have spoken of second Calathumpians; but of course he has no means of knowing how unlike herself she is when in his company.

To go back to our first Sunday worship in Edinburgh. The church officer closed the door of the pulpit on the Reverend Ronald, and I thought I heard the clicking of a lock; at all events, he returned at the close of the services to liberate him and escort him back to the vestry; for the entrances and exits of this beadle, or "minister's man," as the church officer is called in the country districts, form an impressive part of the ceremonies. If he did lock the minister into the pulpit, it is probably only another national custom, like the occasional locking in of the passengers in a railway train, and may be positively necessary in the case of such magnetic and popular preachers as Mr. Macdonald or the Friar.

I have never seen such attention, such concentration, as in these great congregations of the Edinburgh churches. As nearly as I can judge, it is intellectual rather than emotional; but it is not a tribute paid to eloquence alone, it is habitual and universal, and is yielded loyally to insufferable dullness when occasion demands.

When the text is announced, there is an indescribable rhythmic movement forward, followed by a concerted rustle of Bible leaves; not the rustle of a few Bibles in a few pious pews, but the rustle of all of them in all the pews, — and there are more Bibles in an Edinburgh Presbyterian church than one ever sees anywhere else, unless it be in the warehouses of the Bible Societies.

The text is read twice clearly, and another rhythmic movement follows when the books are replaced on the shelves. Then there is a delightful settling back of the entire congregation, a snuggling comfortably into corners and a fitting of shoulders to the pews, — not to sleep, however; an older generation may have done that under the strain of a two-hour "wearifu' dreich" sermon, but these church-goers are not to be caught napping. They wear, on the contrary, a keen, expectant, critical look, which must be inexpressibly encouraging to the minister, if he has anything to say. If he has not (and this is a possibility in Edinburgh, as it is everywhere else), then I am sure it is wisdom for the beadle to lock him in, lest he flee when he meets those searching eyes.

The Edinburgh sermon, though doubtless softened in outline in these later years, is still a more carefully built discourse than one ordinarily hears out of Scotland, being constructed on conventional lines of doctrine, exposition, logical inference, and practical application. Though modern preachers do not announce the division of their subject into heads and sub-heads, firstlies and secondlies and finallies my brethren, there seems to be the old framework underneath the sermon, and every one recognizes it as moving silently below the surface; at least, I always fancy that as the minister finishes one point and attacks another the younger folk fix their eagle eyes on him afresh, and the whole congregation sits up straighter and listens more intently, as if making mental notes. They do not listen so much as if they were enthralled, though they often are and have good reason to be, but as if they were to pass an examination on the subject afterwards; and I have no doubt that this is the fact.

The prayers are many, and are divided, apparently, like those of the liturgies, into petitions, confessions, and aspirations; not forgetting the all-embracing one with which we are perfectly familiar in our native land, in which the preacher commends to the Fatherly care every animate and inanimate thing not mentioned specifically in the foregoing supplications. It was in the middle of this compendious petition, "the lang prayer," that rheumatic old Scottish dames used to make a practice of "cheengin' the fit," as they stood devoutly through it. "When the meenister comes to the 'ingetherin' o' the Gentiles,' I ken weel it's time to cheenge legs, for then the prayer is jist half dune," said a good sermon-taster of Fife.

The organ is finding its way rapidly into the Scottish kirks (how can the shade of John Knox endure a "kist o' whistles" in good St. Giles'?), but it is not used yet in some of those we attend most frequently. There is a certain quaint solemnity, a beautiful austerity, in the unaccompanied singing of hymns that touches me profoundly. I am often carried very high on the waves of splendid church music, when the organ's thunder rolls "through vaulted aisles" and the angelic voices of a trained choir chant the aspirations of my soul for me; but when an Edinburgh congregation stands, and the precentor leads in that noble Paraphrase,

> "God of our fathers, be the God
> Of their succeeding race,"

there is a certain ascetic fervor in it that seems to me the perfection of worship. It may be that my Puritan ancestors are mainly responsible for this feeling, or perhaps my recently adopted Jenny Geddes is a factor in it; of course, if she were in the habit of flinging fauldstules at Deans, she was probably the friend of truth and the foe of beauty, so far as it was in her power to separate them.

There is no music during the offertory in these churches, and this, too, pleases my sense of the fitness of things. It cannot soften the woe of the people who are disinclined to the giving away of money, and the cheerful givers need no encouragement. For my part, I like to sit, quite undistracted by soprano solos, and listen to the refined tinkle of the sixpences and shillings, and the vulgar chink of the pennies and ha'pennies, in the contribution-boxes. Country ministers, I am told, develop such an acute sense of hearing that they can estimate the amount of the collection before it is counted. There is often a huge pewter plate just within the church door, in which the offerings are placed as the worshipers enter or leave; and one always notes the preponderance of silver at the morning, and of copper at the evening services. It is perhaps needless to say that before Francesca had been in Edinburgh a fortnight she asked Mr. Macdonald if it were true that the Scots continued coining the farthing for years and years, merely to have a piece of money serviceable for church offerings!

As to social differences in the congregations we are somewhat at sea. We tried to arrive at a conclusion by the hats and bonnets, than which there is usually no more infallible test. On our first Sunday we attended the Free Kirk in the morning, and the Established in the evening. The bonnets of the Free Kirk were so much the more elegant that we said to one another, "This is evidently the church of society, though the adjective 'Free' should by rights attract the masses." On the second Sunday we reversed the order of things, and found the Established bonnet much finer than the Free bonnets, which was a source of mystification to us, until we discovered that it was a question of morning or evening service, not of the form of Presbyterianism. We think, on the whole, that, taking town and country congregations together, millinery has not flourished under Presbyterianism, — it seems to thrive better in the Romish atmosphere of France; but the Disruption, at least, has had nothing to answer for in the matter, as it appears simply to have parted the bonnets of Scotland in twain, as Moses divided the Red Sea, and left good and evil on both sides.

I can never forget our first military service at St. Giles'. We left Breadalbane Terrace before nine in the morning and walked along the beautiful curve of street that sweeps around the base of Castle Rock, — walked on through the poverty and squalor of the High Street, keeping in view the beautiful lantern tower as a guiding star, till we heard

> "The murmur of the city crowd;
> And, from his steeple, jingling loud,
> St. Giles's mingling din."

We joined the throng outside the venerable church, and awaited the approach of the soldiers from the Castle parade-ground; for it is from there they march in detachments to the church of their choice. A religion they must have, and if, when called up and questioned about it, they have forgotten to provide themselves, or have no preference as to form of worship, they are assigned to one by the person in authority. When the regiments are assembled on the parade-ground of a Sunday morning, the first command is, "Church of Scotland, right about face, quick march!" — the bodies of men belonging to other denominations standing fast until their turn comes to move. It is said that a new officer once gave the command, " Church of Scotland, right about face, quick march ! Fancy releegions, stay where ye are ! "

Just as we were being told this story by an attendant squire, there was a burst of scarlet and a blare of music, and down Castle Hill and the Lawnmarket into Parliament Square marched hundreds of redcoats, the Highland pipers (otherwise the Olympian gods) swinging in front, leaving the American female heart prostrate beneath their victorious tread. The strains of music that in the distance sounded so martial and triumphant we recognized in a moment as "Abide with me," and never did the fine old tune seem more majestic than when it marked a measure for the steady tramp, tramp, tramp, of those soldierly feet. As "The March of the Cameron Men," piped from the green steeps of Castle Hill, had aroused in us thoughts of splendid victories on the battlefield, so did this simple hymn awake the spirit of the church militant ; a no less stern, but more spiritual soldiership, in which "the fruit of righteousness is sown in peace of them that make peace."

As I fell asleep on that first Sunday night in Edinburgh, after the somewhat unusual experience of three church services in a single day, three separate notes of memory floated in and out of the fabric of my dreams : the sound of the soldiers' feet marching into old St. Giles' to the strains of " Abide with me ; " the voice of the Reverend Ronald ringing out with manly insistence : " It is aspiration that counts, not realization ; pursuit, not achievement ; quest, not conquest ! " — and the closing phrases of the Friar's prayer : " When Christ has forgiven us, help us to forgive ourselves ! Help us to forgive ourselves so fully that we can even forget ourselves, remembering only Him ! And so let his kingdom come ; we ask it for the King's sake, Amen."

X

EVEN at this time of Assemblies, when the atmosphere is almost exclusively clerical and ecclesiastical, the two great church armies represented here certainly conceal from the casual observer all rivalries and jealousies, if indeed they cherish any. As for the two dissenting bodies, the Church of the Disruption and the Church of the Secession have been keeping company, so to speak, for some years, with a distant eye to an eventual union. In the light of all this pleasant toleration, it seems difficult to realize that earlier Edinburgh, where, we learned from old parochial records of 1605, Margaret Sinclair was cited by the Session of the Kirk for being at the Burne for water on the Sabbath; that Janet Merling was ordered to make public repentance for concealing a bairn unbaptized in her house for the space of twenty weeks and calling said bairn Janet; that Pat Richardson had to crave mercy for being found in his boat in time of afternoon service; and that Janet Walker, accused of having visitors in her house in sermon-time, had to confess her offense and on her knees crave mercy of God *and* the Kirk Session (which no doubt was much worse) under penalty of a hundred pounds Scots. Possibly there are people yet who would prefer to pay a hundred pounds rather than hear a sermon, but they are few.

It was in the early seventeen hundred and thirties when Allan Ramsay, "in fear and trembling of legal and clerical censure," lent out the plays of Congreve and Farquhar from his famous High Street library. In 1756 it was that the Presbytery of Edinburgh suspended all clergymen who had witnessed the representation of "Douglas," that virtuous tragedy written, to the dismay of all Scotland, by a minister of the Kirk. That the world, even the theological world, moves with tolerable rapidity when once set in motion, is evinced by the fact that on Mrs. Siddons' second engagement in Edinburgh, in the summer of 1785, vast crowds gathered about the doors of the theatre, not at night alone, but in the day, to secure places. It became necessary to admit them first at three in the afternoon, and then at noon, and eventually "the General Assembly of the Church then in session was compelled to arrange its meetings with reference to the appearance of the great actress." How one would have enjoyed hearing that Scotsman say, after one of her most splendid flights of tragic passion, "That's no bad!" We have read of her dismay at this ludicrous parsimony of praise, but her self-respect must have been restored when the Edinburgh ladies fainted by dozens during her impersonation of Isabella in "The Fatal Marriage."

Since Scottish hospitality is well-nigh inexhaustible, it is not strange that from the moment Edinburgh streets began to be crowded with ministers, our drawing-room table began to bear shoals of engraved invitations of every conceivable sort, all equally unfamiliar to our American eyes.

"The Purse-Bearer is commanded by the Lord High Commissioner and the Marchioness of Heatherdale to invite Miss Hamilton to a Garden Party at the Palace of Holyrood House, on the 27th of May. *Weather permitting.*"

"The General Assembly of the Free Church of Scotland admits Miss Hamilton to any gallery on any day."

"The Marchioness of Heatherdale is At Home on the 26th of May from a quarter past nine in the evening. Palace of Holyrood House."

"The Moderator of the General Assembly of the Free Church of Scotland is At Home in the Library of the New College on Saturday, the 22d May, from eight to ten in the evening."

"The Moderator asks the pleasure of Miss Hamilton's presence at a Breakfast to be given on the morning of the 25th of May at Dunedin Hotel."

We determined to go to all these functions

impartially, tracking thus the Presbyterian lion to his very lair, and observing his home as well as his company manners. In everything that related to the distinctively religious side of the proceedings we sought advice from Mrs. M'Collop, while we went to Lady Baird for definite information on secular matters. We also found an unexpected ally in the person of our own ex-Moderator's niece, Miss Jean Dalziel (Deeyell). She has been educated in Paris, but she must always have been a delightfully breezy person, quite too irrepressible to be affected by Scottish *haar* or theology. "Go to the Assemblies, by all means," she said, "and be sure and get places for the heresy case. These are no longer what they once were, — we are getting lamentably weak and gelatinous in our beliefs, — but there is an unusually nice one this year; the heretic is very young and handsome, and quite wicked, as ministers go. Don't fail to be presented at the Marchioness's court at Holyrood, for it is a capital preparation for the ordeal of Her Majesty and Buckingham Palace. 'Nothing fit to wear'? You have never seen the people who go, or you would n't say that! I even advise you to attend one of the breakfasts; it can't do you any serious or permanent injury so long as you eat something before you go. Oh no, it does n't matter, — whichever one you choose, you will cheerfully omit the other; for I avow as a Scottish spinster, and the niece of an ex-Moderator, that to a stranger and a foreigner the breakfasts are worse than Arctic explorations. If you do not chance to be at the table of honor " —

" The gifted Miss Hamilton is always at the table of honor; unless she is placed there she refuses to eat, and then the universe rocks to its centre," interpolated Francesca impertinently.

" It is true," continued Miss Dalziel, "you will often sit beside a minister or a minister's wife, who will make you scorn the sordid appetites of flesh, but if you do not, then eat as little as may be, and flee up the Mound to whichever Assembly is the Mecca of your soul ! "

" My niece's tongue is an unruly member," said the ex-Moderator, who was present at this diatribe, " and the principal mistake she makes in her judgment of these clerical feasts is that she criticises them as conventional repasts, whereas they are intended to be informal meetings together of people who wish to be better acquainted."

" Hot bacon and eggs would be no bar to friendship," answered Miss Dalziel, with an affectionate *moue.*

" Cold bacon and eggs is better than cold piety," said the ex-Moderator, " and it may be a good discipline for fastidious young ladies who have been spoiled by Parisian breakfasts."

It is to Mrs. M'Collop that we owe our chief

insight into technical church matters, although we seldom agree with her "opeenions" after we gain our own experience. She never misses hearing one sermon on a Sabbath, and oftener she listens to two or three. Neither does she confine herself to the ministrations of a single preacher, but roves from one sanctuary to another, seeking the bread of life, often, however, according to her own account, getting a particularly indigestible "stane."

She is thus a complete guide to the Edinburgh pulpit, and when she is making a bed in the morning she dispenses criticism in so large and impartial a manner that it would make the flesh of the "meenistry" creep were it overheard. I used to think Ian Maclaren's sermon-taster a possible exaggeration of an existent type, but I now see that she is truth itself.

"Ye'll be tryin' anither kirk the morn?" suggests Mrs. M'Collop, spreading the clean Sunday sheet over the mattress. "Wha did ye hear the Sawbath that's bye? Dr. A? Ay, I ken him ower weel; he's been there for fifteen years an' mair. Ay, he's a gifted mon — *off an' on!*" with an emphasis showing clearly that, in her estimation, the times when he is "off" outnumber those when he is "on." . . . "Ye have na heard auld Dr. B yet?" (Here she tucks in the upper sheet tidily at the foot.) "He's a graund strachtforrit mon, is Dr. B, forbye he's growin' maist awfu' dreich in his sermons, though when he's that wearisome a body canna heed him wi'-oot takin' peppermints to the kirk, he's nane the less, at seeventy-sax, a better mon than the new asseestant. Div ye ken the new asseestant? He's a wee-bit, finger-fed mannie, ower sma' maist to wear a goon! I canna thole him, wi' his lang-nebbit words, explainin' an' expoundin' the gude Book as if it had jist come oot! The auld doctor's nae kirk-filler, but he gies us fu' meesure, pressed doun an' rinnin' over, nae bit-pickin's like the haverin' asseestant; it's my opeenion he's no soond, wi' his parleyvoos an' his clishmaclavers! . . . Mr. C?" (Now comes the shaking and straightening and smoothing of the first blanket.) "Ay, he's weel eneuch! I mind ance he prayed for our Free Assembly, an' then he turned roun' an' prayed for the Estaiblished, maist in the same breath, — he's a broad, leeberal mon is Mr. C! . . . Mr. D? Ay, I ken him fine; he micht be waur, though he's ower fond o' the kittle pairts o' the Old Testament; but he reads his sermon from the paper, an' it's an auld sayin', 'If a meenister canna mind [remember] his ain discoorse, nae mair can the congregation be expectit to mind it.' . . . Mr. E? He's my ain meenister." (She has a pillow in her mouth now, but though she is shaking it as a terrier would a rat, and drawing on the linen slip at the same time, she is still intelligible between the jerks.) "Susanna says his sermon is like claith made o' soond 'oo [wool] wi' a gude twined thread, an' wairpit an' weftit wi' doctrine. Susanna kens her Bible weel, but she's never gaed forrit." (To "gang forrit" is to take the communion.) "Dr. F? I ca' him the greetin' doctor! He's aye dingin' the dust oot o' the poopit cushions, an' greetin' ower the sins o' the human race, an' eespecially of his ain congregation. He's waur syne his last wife sickened an' slippit awa.' 'T was a chastenin' he'd put up wi' twice afore, but he grat nane the less. She was a bonnie bit body, was the thurd Mistress F! E'nbro could 'a' better spared the greetin' doctor than her, I'm thinkin'."

"The Lord giveth and the Lord taketh away, according to his good will and pleasure," I ventured piously, as Mrs. M'Collop beat the bolster and laid it in place.

"Ou ay," responded that good woman, as she spread the counterpane over the pillows in the way I particularly dislike — "ou ay, but whiles I think it's a peety he couldna be guidit!"

XI

WE were to make our bow to the Lord High Commissioner and the Marchioness of Heatherdale in the evening, and we were in a state of republican excitement at 22, Breadalbane Terrace.

Francesca had surprised us by refusing to be presented at this semi-royal Scottish court. "Not I," she said. "The Marchioness represents the Queen; we may discover, when we arrive, that she has raised the standards of admission, and requires us to 'back out' of the throne-room. I don't propose to do that without London training. Besides, I detest crowds, and I never go to my own President's receptions; and I have a headache, anyway, and I don't feel like coping with the Reverend Ronald to-night!" (Lady Baird was to take us under her wing, and her nephew was to escort us, Sir Robert being in Inveraray.)

"Sally, my dear," I said, as Francesca left the room with a bottle of smelling-salts somewhat ostentatiously in evidence, "methinks the damsel doth protest too much. In other words, she devotes a good deal of time and discussion to a gentleman whom she heartily dislikes. As she is under your care, I will direct your attention to the following points : —

"Ronald Macdonald is a Scotsman; Francesca disapproves of international alliances.

"He is a Presbyterian; she is a Swedenborgian.

"His father was a famous old school doctor; Francesca is a homœopathist.

"He is serious; Francesca is gay.

"I think, under all the circumstances, their acquaintance will bear watching. Two persons so utterly dissimilar, and, so far as superficial observation goes, so entirely unsuited to each other, are quite likely to drift into marriage unless diverted by watchful philanthropists."

"Nonsense!" returned Salemina brusquely. "You think because you are under the spell of the tender passion yourself that other people are in constant danger. Francesca detests him."

"Who told you so?"

"She herself," triumphantly.

"Salemina," I said pityingly, "I have always believed you a spinster from choice; don't lead me to think that you have never had any experience in these matters! The Reverend Ronald has also intimated to me as plainly as he dared that he cannot bear the sight of Francesca. What do I gather from this statement? The general conclusion that if it be true, it is curious that he looks at her incessantly."

"Francesca would never live in Scotland," remarked Salemina feebly.

"Not unless she were asked, of course," I replied.

"He would never ask her."

"Not unless he thought he had a chance of an affirmative answer."

"Her father would never allow it."

"Her father allows what she permits him to allow. You know that perfectly well."

"What shall I do about it, then?"

"Consult me."

"What shall *we* do about it?"

"Let Nature have her own way."

"I don't believe in Nature."

"Don't be profane, Salemina, and don't be unromantic, which is worse; but if you insist, trust in Providence."

"I would rather trust Francesca's hard heart."

"The hardest hearts melt if sufficient heat be applied. Did I take you to Newhaven and read you 'Christie Johnstone' on the beach for naught? Don't you remember Charles Reade said that the Scotch are icebergs, with volcanoes underneath; thaw the Scotch ice, which is very cold, and you shall get to the Scotch fire, warmer than any sun of Italy or Spain. I think Mr. Macdonald is a volcano."

"I wish he were extinct," said Salemina petulantly, "and I wish you would n't make me nervous."

"If you had any faculty of premonition, you would n't have waited for me to make you nervous."

"Some people are singularly omniscient."

"Others are singularly deficient "— And at this moment Susanna Crum came in to announce Miss Jean Dalziel, who had come to see sights with us.

It was our almost daily practice to walk through the Old Town, and we were now familiar with every street and close in that densely crowded quarter. Our quest for the sites of ancient landmarks never grew monotonous, and we were always reconstructing, in imagination, the Cowgate, the Canongate, the Lawnmarket, and the High Street, until we could see Auld Reekie as it was in bygone centuries. In those days of continual war with England, people crowded their dwellings as near the Castle as possible, so floor was piled upon floor and flat upon flat, families ensconcing themselves above other families, the tendency being ever skyward. Those who dwelt on top had no desire to spend their strength in carrying down the corkscrew stairs matter which would descend by the force of gravity if pitched from the window or door; so the wayfarer, especially after dusk, would be greeted with cries of "Get out o' the gait!" or "Gardy loo!" which was in the French "*Gardez l'eau*," and which would have been understood in any language, I fancy, after a little experience. The streets then were filled with the débris flung from a hundred upper windows, while certain ground-floor tenants, such as butchers and candlemakers, contributed their full share to the fragrant heaps. As for these too seldom used narrow turnpike stairs, imagine the dames of fashion tilting their vast hoops and silken show-petticoats up and down in them!

That swine roamed at will in these Elysian fields is to be presumed, since we have this amusing picture of three High Street belles and beauties in the "Traditions of Edinburgh:"—

"So easy were the manners of the great, fabled to be so stiff and decorous," says the author, "that Lady Maxwell's daughter Jane, who afterward became the Duchess of Gordon, was seen riding a sow up the High Street, while her sister Eglantine (afterwards Lady Wallace of Craigie) thumped lustily behind with a stick."

No wonder, in view of all this, that King James VI., when about to bring home his "darrest spous" Anne of Denmark, wrote to the Provost, "For God's sake see a' things are richt at our hame-coming; a king with a new-married wife doesna come hame ilka day."

Had it not been for these royal home-comings and visits of distinguished foreigners, now and again aided by something still more salutary, an occasional outbreak of the plague, the easy-going authorities would never have issued any "cleansing edicts," and the still easier-going inhabitants would never have obeyed them. It was these dark, tortuous wynds and closes, nevertheless, that made up the Court End of Old Edinbro'; for some one writes in 1530, "Via vaccarum in quâ habitant patricii et senatores urbis" (The nobility and chief senators of the city dwell in the Cowgate). And as for the Canongate, this Saxon *gaet* or way of the Holyrood canons, it still sheltered in 1753 "two dukes, sixteen earls, two dowager countesses, seven lords, seven lords of session, thirteen baronets, four commanders of the forces in Scotland, and five eminent men," — fine game indeed for Mally Lee!

> "A' doun alang the Canongate
>   Were beaux o' ilk degree;
> And mony ane turned round to look
>   At bonny Mally Lee.
> And we 're a' gaun east an' west,
>   We 're a' gaun agee,
> We 're a' gaun east an' west
>   Courtin' Mally Lee!"

Every corner bristles with memories. Here is the Stamp Office Close, from which the lovely Susanna, Countess of Eglinton, was wont to issue on Assembly nights; she, six feet in height, with a brilliantly fair complexion and a "face of the maist bewitching loveliness." Her seven daughters and stepdaughters were all conspicuously handsome, and it was deemed a goodly sight to watch the long procession of eight gilded sedan-chairs pass from the Stamp Office Close, bearing her and her stately brood to the Assembly Room, amid a crowd that was "hushed with respect and admiration to behold their lofty and graceful figures step from the chairs on the pavement."

Here itself is the site of those old Assemblies presided over at one time by the famous Miss Nicky Murray, a directress of society affairs, who seems to have been a feminine premonition of Count d'Orsay and our own McAllister. Rather dull they must have been, those old Scotch balls, where Goldsmith saw the ladies and gentlemen in two dismal groups divided by the length of the room.

> "The Assembly Close received the fair —
> Order and elegance presided there —
> Each gay Right Honourable had her place,
> To walk a minuet with becoming grace.
> No racing to the dance with rival hurry,
> Such was thy sway, O famed Miss Nicky Murray!"

It was half past nine in the evening when Salemina and I drove to Holyrood, our humble cab-horse jogging faithfully behind Lady Baird's brougham, and it was the new experience of seeing Auld Reekie by lamplight that called up these gay visions of other days, — visions and days so thoroughly our mental property that we could not help resenting the fact that women were hanging washing from the Countess of Eglinton's former windows, and popping their unkempt heads out of the Duchess of Gordon's old doorway.

The Reverend Ronald is so kind! He enters so fully into our spirit of inquiry, and takes such pleasure in our enthusiasms! He even sprang lightly out of Lady Baird's carriage and called to our "lamiter" to halt while he showed us the site of the Black Turnpike, from whose windows Queen Mary saw the last of her kingdom's capital.

"Here was the Black Turnpike, Miss Hamilton!" he cried; "and from here Mary went to Loch Leven, where you Hamiltons and the Setons came gallantly to her help. Don't you remember the 'far ride to the Solway sands'?"

I looked with interest, though I was in such a state of delicious excitement that I could scarce keep my seat.

"Only a few minutes more, Salemina," I sighed, "and we shall be in the palace courtyard; then a probable half-hour in crowded dressing-rooms, with another half-hour in line, and then, then we shall be making our best republican bow in the Gallery of the Kings! How I wish Mr. Beresford and Francesca were with us! What do you suppose was her real reason for staying away? Some petty disagreement with our young minister, I am sure. Do you think the dampness is taking the curl out of our hair? Do you suppose our gowns will be torn to ribbons before the Marchioness sees them? Do you believe we shall look as well as anybody? Privately, I think we must look better than anybody; but I always think that on my way to a party, never after I arrive."

Mrs. M'Collop had asserted that I was "bonnie eneuch for ony court," and I could not help wishing that "mine ain dear Somebody" might see me in my French frock embroidered with silver thistles, and my "shower bouquet" of Scottish bluebells tied loosely together. Salemina wore pinky-purple velvet; a real heather color it was, though the Lord High Commissioner would probably never note the fact.

When we had presented our cards of invitation at the palace doors, we joined the throng and patiently made our way up the splendid staircases, past powdered lackeys without number, and, divested of our wraps, joined another throng on our way to the throne-room, Salemina and I pressing those cards with our names "legibly written on them" close to our palpitating breasts.

At last the moment came when, Lady Baird having preceded me, I handed my bit of pasteboard to the usher; and hearing "Miss Hamilton" called in stentorian accents, I went forward in my turn, and executed a graceful and elegant but not too profound curtsy, carefully arranged to suit the semi-royal, semi-ecclesiastical occasion. I had not divulged the fact even to Salemina, but I had worn Mrs. M'Collop's carpet quite threadbare in front of the long mirror, and had curtsied to myself so many times in its crystal surface that I had developed a sort of fictitious reverence for my reflected image. I had only begun my well-practiced obeisance when Her Grace the Marchioness, to my mingled surprise and embarrassment, extended a gracious hand and murmured my name in a particularly kind voice. She is fond of Lady Baird, and perhaps chose this method of showing her friendship; or it may be that she noticed my silver thistles and Salemina's heather-colored velvet, — they certainly deserved special recognition; or it may be that I was too beautiful to pass over in silence, — in my state of exaltation I was quite equal to the belief.

The presentation over, we wandered through the spacious apartments, leaning from the open windows to hear the music of the band playing in the courtyard below, looking at the royal portraits, and chatting with groups of friends who appeared and reappeared in the throng. Finally Lady Baird sent for us to join her in a knot of personages more and less distinguished, who had dined at the palace, and who were standing behind the receiving party in a sort of sacred group. This indeed was a ground of vantage, and one could have stood there for hours, watching all sorts and conditions of men and women bowing before the Lord High Commissioner and the Marchioness, who, with her Cleopatra-like beauty and scarlet gown, looked like a gorgeous cardinal-flower.

Salemina and I watched the curtsying narrowly, with the view at first of improving our own obeisances for Buckingham Palace; but truth to say we got no added light, and plainly most of the people had not worn threadbare the carpets in front of their dressing-mirrors.

Suddenly we heard a familiar name announced, "Lord Colquhoun," a distinguished judge who had lately been raised to the peerage, and whom we often met at dinners; then "Miss Rowena Colquhoun;" and then, in the midst, we fancied, of an unusual stir at the entrance door — "Miss Francesca Van Buren Monroe." I involuntarily touched the Reverend Ronald's shoulder in my astonishment, while Salemina lifted her tortoise-shell lorgnette, and we gazed silently at our recreant charge.

After presentation, each person has fifteen or twenty feet of awful space to traverse in solitary and defenseless majesty; scanned meanwhile by the maids of honor (who, if they were truly honorable, would turn their eyes another way), ladies-in-waiting, the sacred group in the rear, and the Purse-Bearer himself. I had supposed that this functionary would keep the purse in his upper bureau drawer at home, when he was not paying bills, but it seems that when on processional duty he carries a bag of red velvet quite a yard long over his arm, where it looks not unlike a lady's opera-cloak. It would hold the sum total of the moneys disbursed, even if they were reduced to the standard of vulgar copper.

Under this appalling fire of inspection, some of the victims waddle, some hurry; some look up and down nervously, others glance over the shoulder as if dreading to be apprehended; some turn red, others pale, according to complexion and temperament; some swing their arms, others trip on their gowns; some twitch the buttons of a glove, or tweak a flower or a jewel. Francesca rose superior to all these weaknesses, and I doubt if the Gallery of the Kings ever served as a background for anything lovelier or more highbred than that untitled slip of a girl from "the States." Her trailing gown of pearl-white satin fell in unbroken lustrous folds behind her. Her beautiful throat and shoulders rose in statuesque whiteness from the mist of chiffon that encircled them. Her dark hair showed a moonbeam parting that rested the eye, wearied by the contemplation of waves and frizzes fresh from the curling-tongs. Her mother's pearls hung in ropes from neck to waist, and the one spot of color about her was the single American Beauty rose she carried. There is a patriotic florist in Paris who grows these long-stemmed empresses of the rose-garden, and Mr. Beresford sends some to me every week. Francesca had taken the flower without permission, and I must say she was as worthy of it as it of her.

She curtsied deeply, with no exaggerated ceremony, but with a sort of innocent and childlike gravity, while the satin of her gown spread itself like a great blossom over the floor. Her head was bowed until the dark lashes swept her crimson cheeks; then she rose again from the heart of the shimmering lily, with the one splendid rose glowing against all her dazzling whiteness, and floated slowly across the dreaded space to the door of exit as if she were preceded by invisible heralds and followed by invisible train-bearers.

"Who is she?" we heard whispered here and there. "Look at the rose!" "Look at the pearls! Is she a princess or only an American?"

I glanced at the Reverend Ronald. I imagined he looked pale; at any rate, he was biting his under lip nervously and I believe he was in fancy laying his serious, Scottish, allopathic, Presbyterian heart at Francesca's gay, American, homœopathic, Swedenborgian feet.

"It is a pity Miss Monroe is such an ardent republican," he said, with unconcealed bitterness; "otherwise she ought to be a duchess. I never saw a head that better suited a coronet, nor, if you will pardon me, one that contained more caprices."

"It is true she flatly refused to accompany us here," I allowed, "but perhaps she has some explanation more or less silly and serviceable; meantime, I defy you to tell me she isn't a beauty, and I implore you to say nothing about its being only skin-deep. Give me a beautiful exterior, say I, and I will spend my life in making the hidden things of mind and soul conform to it; but deliver me from all forlorn attempts to make my beauty of character speak through a large mouth, breathe through a fat nose, and look at my neighbor through crossed eyes!"

Mr. Macdonald agreed with me, with some few ministerial reservations. He always agrees with me, and why he is not tortured at the thought of my being the promised bride of another, but continues to squander his affections upon a quarrelsome and unappreciative girl, is more than I can comprehend.

Francesca, escorted by Lord Colquhoun, appeared presently in our group, but Salemina did not even attempt to scold her. One cannot scold an imperious young beauty in white satin and pearls, particularly if she is leaning nonchalantly on the arm of a peer of the realm.

It seems that shortly after our departure (we had dined with Lady Baird) Lord Colquhoun had sent a note to me, requiring an answer. Francesca had opened it, and found that he offered an extra card of invitation to one of us, and said that he and his sister would gladly serve as escort to Holyrood, if desired. She had had an hour or two of solitude by this time, and was well weary of it, while the last vestige of headache disappeared under the temptation of appearing at court with all the éclat of unexpectedness. She dispatched a note of acceptance to Lord Colquhoun, summoned Mrs. M'Collop, Susanna, and the maiden Boots to her assistance, spread the trays of her Saratoga trunks about our three bedrooms, grouped all our candles on her dressing-table, and borrowed any little elegance of toilette which we chanced to have left behind. Her own store of adornments is much greater than ours, but we possess certain articles for which she has a childlike admiration: my white satin slippers embroidered with seed pearls, Salemina's pearl-topped comb, Salemina's Valenciennes handkerchief and diamond belt-clasp, my pearl frog with ruby eyes. We identified our property on her impertinent young person, and the list of her borrowings so amused the Reverend Ronald that he forgot his injuries.

"It is really an ordeal, that presentation, no matter how strong one's sense of humor may be, nor how well rooted one's democracy," chattered Francesca to a serried rank of officers who surrounded her to the total routing of the ministry. "It is especially trying if one has come unexpectedly and has no idea of what is to happen.

I was agitated at the supreme moment, because, at the entrance of the throne-room, I had just shaken hands reverently with a splendid person who proved to be a footman. Of course I took him for the Commander of the Queen's Guards, or the Keeper of the Dungeon Keys, or the Most Noble Custodian of the Royal Moats, Drawbridges, and Portcullises. When he put out his hand I had no idea it was simply to waft me onward, and so naturally I shook it, — it's a mercy that I did n't kiss it! Then I curtsied to the Royal Usher, and overlooked the Lord High Commissioner altogether, having no eyes for any one but the beautiful scarlet Marchioness. I only hope they were too busy to notice my mistakes, otherwise I shall be banished from Court at the very moment of my presentation. — Do you still banish nowadays?" turning the battery of her eyes upon a particularly insignificant officer who was far too dazed to answer. "Did you see the child of ten who was next to me in line? She is Mrs. Macstronachlacher; at least that was the name on the card she carried, and she was thus announced. As they tell us the Purse-Bearer is most rigorous in arranging these functions and issuing the invitations, I presume she must be Mrs. Macstronachlacher; but if so, they marry very young in Scotland, and her skirts should really have been longer!"

XII

It is our last day in "Scotia's darling seat," our last day in Breadalbane Terrace, our last day with Mrs. M'Collop; and though every one says that we shall love the life in the country, we are loath to leave Auld Reekie.

Salemina and I have spent two days in search of an abiding-place, and have visited eight well-recommended villages with that end in view; but she disliked four of them, and I could n't endure the other four, though I considered some of those that fell under her disapproval as quite delightful in every respect.

We never take Francesca on these pilgrimages of disagreement, as three conflicting opinions on the same subject would make insupportable what is otherwise rather exhilarating. She starts from Edinburgh to-morrow for a brief visit to the Highlands with the Dalziels, and will join us when we have settled ourselves.

Mr. Beresford leaves Paris as soon after our decision as he is permitted, so Salemina and I have agreed to agree upon one ideal spot within thirty-six hours of our quitting Edinburgh, knowing privately that after a last battle royal we shall enthusiastically support the joint decision for the rest of our lives.

We have been bidding good-by to people and places and things, and wishing the sun would not shine and thus make our task the harder. We have looked our last on the old gray town from Calton Hill, of all places the best, perhaps, for a view; since, as Stevenson says, from Calton Hill you can see the Castle, which you lose from the Castle, and Arthur's Seat, which you cannot see from Arthur's Seat. We have taken a farewell walk to the Dean Bridge, to gaze wistfully eastward and marvel for the hundredth time to find so beautiful a spot in the heart of a city. The soft flowing Water of Leith winding over pebbles between grassy banks and groups of splendid trees, the roof of the little temple to Hygeia rising picturesquely among green branches, the slopes of emerald velvet leading up to the gray stone of the houses, — where, in all the world of cities, can one find a view to equal it in peaceful loveliness? Francesca's "bridge-man," who, by the way, proved to be a distinguished young professor of medicine in the university, says that the beautiful cities of the world should be ranked thus, — Constantinople, Prague, Genoa, Edinburgh; but having seen only one of these, and that the last, I refuse to credit any sliding scale of comparison which leaves Edina at the foot.

It was nearing tea-time, an hour when we never fail to have visitors, and we were all in the drawing-room together. I was at the piano, singing

Jacobite melodies for Salemina's delectation. When I came to the last verse of Lady Nairne's "Hundred Pipers," the spirited words had taken my fancy captive, and I am sure I could not have sung with more vigor and passion had my people been " out with the Chevalier."

> " The Esk was swollen sae red an' sae deep,
> But shouther to shouther the brave lads keep ;
> Twa thousand swam oure to fell English ground,
> An' danced themselves dry to the pibroch's sound.
> Dumfounder'd the English saw, they saw,
> Dumfounder'd they heard the blaw, the blaw,
> Dumfounder'd they a' ran awa', awa',
> Frae the hundred pipers an' a', an' a' ! "

By the time I came to " Dumfounder'd the English saw " Francesca left her book and joined in the next four lines, and when we broke into the chorus Salemina rushed to the piano, and although she cannot sing, she lifted her voice both high and loud in the refrain, beating time the while with a dirk paper-knife.

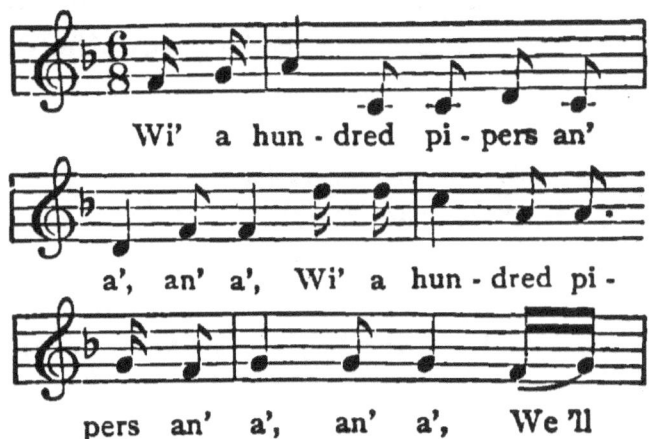

up an' gie them a blaw, a blaw, Wi' a hundred pi-pers an' a', an' a'!

Susanna ushered in Mr. Macdonald and Dr. Moncrieffe as the last "blaw" faded into silence, and Jean Dalziel came upstairs to say that they could seldom get a quiet moment for family prayers, because we were always at the piano, hurling incendiary sentiments into the air, — sentiments set to such stirring melodies that no one could resist them.

"We are very sorry, Miss Dalziel," I said penitently. "We reserve an hour in the morning and another at bedtime for your uncle's prayers, but we had no idea you had them at afternoon tea, even in Scotland. I believe that you are chaffing, and came up only to swell the chorus. Come, let us all sing together from 'Dumfounder'd the English saw.'"

Mr. Macdonald and Dr. Moncrieffe gave such splendid body to the music, and Jean such warlike energy, that Salemina waved her paper-knife in a manner more than ever sanguinary, and Susanna hesitated outside the door for sheer delight, and had to be coaxed in with the tea-things. On the heels of the tea-things came the Dominie, another dear old friend of six weeks' standing; and while the doctor sang "Jock o' Hazledean" with such irresistible charm that we all longed to elope with somebody on the instant, Salemina dispensed buttered toast, marmalade sandwiches, and the fragrant cup. By this time we were thoroughly cosy, and Mr. Macdonald made himself and us very much at home by stirring the fire; whereupon Francesca embarrassed him by begging him not to touch it unless he could do it properly, which, she added, seemed quite unlikely, from the way in which he handled the poker.

"What will Edinburgh do without you?" he asked, turning towards us with flattering sadness in his tone. "Who will hear our Scotch stories, never suspecting their hoary old age? Who will ask us questions to which we somehow always know the answers? Who will make us study and reverence anew our own landmarks? Who will keep warm our national and local pride by judicious enthusiasm?"

"I think the national and local pride may be counted on to exist without any artificial stimulants," dryly observed Francesca, whose spirit is not in the least quenched by approaching departure.

"Perhaps," answered the Reverend Ronald; "but at any rate, you, Miss Monroe, will always be able to reflect that you have never been responsible even for its momentary inflation!"

"Is n't it strange that she cannot get on better with that charming fellow?" murmured Salemina, as she passed me the sugar for my second cup.

"If your present symptoms of blindness continue, Salemina," I said, searching for a small lump so as to gain time, "I shall write you a plaintive ballad, buy you a dog, and stand you on a street corner! If you had ever permitted yourself to 'get on' with any man as Francesca is getting on with Mr. Macdonald, you would now be Mrs. — Somebody."

"Do you know, doctor," asked the Dominie, "that Miss Hamilton shed real tears at Holyrood, the other night, when the band played 'Bonnie Charlie's now awa''?"

"They were real," I confessed, "in the sense that they certainly were not crocodile tears; but I am somewhat at a loss to explain them from a sensible, American standpoint. Of course my Jacobitism is purely impersonal, though scarcely more so than yours, at this late day; at least it is merely a poetic sentiment, for which Caroline, Baroness Nairne is mainly responsible. My romantic tears came from a vision of the Bonnie Prince as he entered Holyrood, dressed in his short tartan coat, his scarlet breeches and military boots, the star of St. Andrew on his breast, a blue ribbon over his shoulder, and the famous blue velvet bonnet and white cockade. He must have looked so brave and handsome and hopeful at that moment, and the moment was so sadly brief, that when the band played the plaintive air I kept hearing the words, —

> 'Mony a heart will break in twa,
> Should he no come back again.'

He did come back again to me that evening, and held a phantom levee behind the Marchioness of Heatherdale's shoulder. His 'ghaist' looked bonnie and rosy and confident, yet all the time the band was playing the requiem for his lost cause and buried hopes."

I looked towards the fire to hide the moisture that crept again into my eyes, and my glance fell upon Francesca sitting dreamily on a hassock in front of the cheerful blaze, her chin in the hollow of her palm, and the Reverend Ronald standing on the hearth-rug gazing at her, the poker in his hand, and his heart, I regret to say, in such an exposed position on his sleeve that even Salemina could have seen it had she turned her eyes that way.

Jean Dalziel broke the momentary silence: "I am sure I never hear the last two lines, —

> 'Better lo'ed ye canna be,
> Will ye no come back again?'

without a lump in my throat," and she hummed the lovely melody. "It is all as you say purely impersonal and poetic. My mother is an Englishwoman, but she sings 'Dumfounder'd the English saw, they saw,' with the greatest fire and fury."

XIII

"I THINK I was never so completely under the spell of a country as I am of Scotland." I made this acknowledgment freely, but I knew that it would provoke comment from my compatriots.

"Oh yes, my dear, you have been just as spellbound before, only you don't remember it," replied Salemina promptly. "I have never seen a person more perilously appreciative or receptive than you."

"'Perilously' is just the word," chimed in Francesca delightedly; "when you care for a place you grow porous, as it were, until after a time you are precisely like blotting-paper. Now, there was Italy, for example. After eight weeks in Venice you were completely Venetian, from your fan to the ridiculous little crêpe shawl you wore because an Italian prince had told you that centuries were usually needed to teach a woman how to wear a shawl, but that you had been born with the art, and the shoulders! Anything but a watery street was repulsive to you. Cobblestones? 'Ordinario, dúro, brútto! A gondola? Ah, bellissima! Let me float forever thus!' You bathed your spirit in sunshine and color; I can hear you murmur now, 'O Venezia benedetta! non ti voglio lasciar!'"

"It was just the same when she spent a month in France with the Baroness de Hautenoblesse," continued Salemina. "When she returned to America it is no flattery to say that in dress, attitude, inflection, manner, she was a thorough Parisienne. There was an elegant superficiality and a superficial elegance about her that I can never forget, nor yet her extraordinary volubility in a foreign language, — the fluency with which she expressed her inmost soul on all topics without the aid of a single irregular verb, for these she was never able to acquire; oh, it was wonderful, but there was no affectation about it; she had simply been a kind of blotting-paper, as Miss Monroe says, and France had written itself all over her."

"I don't wish to interfere with anybody's diagnosis," I interposed at the first possible moment, "but perhaps after you 've both finished your psychologic investigation the subject may be allowed to explain herself from the inside, so to speak. I won't deny the spell of Italy, but I think the spell that Scotland casts over one is quite a different thing, more spiritual, more difficult to break. Italy's charm has something physical in it; it is born of blue sky, sunlit waves, soft atmosphere, orange sails and yellow moons, and appeals more to the senses. In Scotland the climate certainly has naught to do with it, but the imagination is somehow made captive.

I am not enthralled by the past of Italy or France, for instance."

"Of course you are not at the present moment," said Francesca, "because you are enthralled by the past of Scotland, and even you cannot be the slave of two pasts at the same time."

"I never was particularly enthralled by Italy's past," I argued with exemplary patience, "but the romance of Scotland has a flavor all its own. I do not quite know the secret of it."

"It's the kilts and the pipes," said Francesca.

"No, the history." (This from Salemina.)

"Or Sir Walter and the literature," suggested Mr. Macdonald.

"Or the songs and ballads," ventured Jean Dalziel.

"There!" I exclaimed triumphantly, "you see for yourselves you have named avenue after avenue along which one's mind is led in charmed subjection. Where can you find battles that kindle your fancy like Falkirk and Flodden and Culloden and Bannockburn? Where a sovereign that attracts, baffles, repels, allures, like Mary Queen of Scots, — and where, tell me where, is there a Pretender like Bonnie Prince Charlie? Think of the spirit in those old Scottish matrons who could sing : —

'I'll sell my rock, I'll sell my reel,
My rippling-kame and spinning-wheel,

> To buy my lad a tartan plaid,
> A braid sword, durk, and white cockade.'"

"Yes," chimed in Salemina when I had finished quoting, " or that other verse that goes, —

> 'I ance had sons, I now hae nane,
> I bare them toiling sairlie;
> But I would bear them a' again
> To lose them a' for Charlie!'

Is n't the enthusiasm almost beyond belief at this distance of time?" she went on; "and is n't it a curious fact, as Mr. Macdonald told me a moment ago, that though the whole country was vocal with songs for the lost cause and the fallen race, not one in favor of the victors ever became popular?"

"Sympathy for the under dog, as Miss Monroe's countrywomen would say picturesquely," remarked Mr. Macdonald.

"I don't see why all the vulgarisms in the dictionary should be foisted on the American girl," retorted Francesca loftily, "unless, indeed, it is a determined attempt to find spots upon the sun for fear we shall worship it!"

"Quite so, quite so!" returned the Reverend Ronald, who has had reason to know that this phrase reduces Miss Monroe to voiceless rage.

"The Stuart charm and personal magnetism must have been a powerful factor in all that movement," said Salemina, plunging hastily back into the topic to avert any further recrimination.

"I suppose we feel it even now, and if I had been alive in 1745 I should probably have made myself ridiculous. 'Old maiden ladies,' I read this morning, 'were the last leal Jacobites in Edinburgh; spinsterhood in its loneliness remained ever true to Prince Charlie and the vanished dreams of youth.'"

"Yes," continued the Dominie, "the story is told of the last of those Jacobite ladies who never failed to close her Prayer-Book and stand erect in silent protest when the prayer for 'King George III. and the reigning family' was read by the congregation."

"Do you remember the prayer of the Reverend Neil McVicar in St. Cuthbert's?" asked Mr. Macdonald. "It was in 1745, after the victory at Prestonpans, when a message was sent to the Edinburgh ministers, in the name of 'Charles, Prince Regent,' desiring them to open their churches next day as usual. McVicar preached to a large congregation, many of whom were armed Highlanders, and prayed for George II., and also for Charles Edward, in the following fashion: 'Bless the king! Thou knowest what king I mean. May the crown sit long upon his head! As for that young man who has come among us to seek an earthly crown, we beseech Thee to take him to Thyself and give him a crown of glory!'"

"Ah, what a pity the Bonnie Prince had not

died after his meteor victory at Falkirk!" exclaimed Jean Dalziel, when we had finished laughing at Mr. Macdonald's story.

"Or at Culloden, 'where, quenched in blood on the Muir of Drummossie, the star of the Stuarts sank forever,'" quoted the Dominie. "There is where his better self died; would that the young Chevalier had died with it! By the way, doctor, we must not sit here eating goodies and sipping tea until the dinner-hour, for these ladies have doubtless much to do for their flitting" (a pretty Scots word for "moving").

"We are quite ready for our flitting so far as packing is concerned," Salemina assured him. "Would that we were as ready in spirit! Miss Hamilton has even written her farewell poem, which I am sure she will read for the asking."

"She will read it without that formality," murmured Francesca. "She has lived and toiled only for this moment, and the poem is in her pocket."

"Delightful!" said the doctor flatteringly. "Has she favored you already? Have you heard it, Miss Monroe?"

"Have we heard it!" ejaculated that young person. "We have heard nothing else all the morning! What you will take for local color is nothing but our mental life-blood, which she has mercilessly drawn to stain her verses. We each tried to write a Scottish poem, and as Miss Hamilton's was better, or perhaps I might say less bad, than ours, we encouraged her to develop and finish it. I wanted to do an imitation of Lindsay's

> 'Adieu, Edinburgh! thou heich triumphant town,
> Within whose bounds richt blithefull have I been!'

but it proved too difficult. Miss Hamilton's general idea was that we should write some verses in good plain English. Then we were to take out all the final *g*'s, and indeed the final letters from all the words wherever it was possible, so that *full, awful, call, ball, hall, and away* should be *fu', awfu', ca', ba', ha', an' awa'*. This alone gives great charm and character to a poem; but we were also to change all words ending in *ow* into *aw*. This does n't injure the verse, you see, as *blaw* and *snaw* rhyme just as well as *blow* and *snow*, beside bringing tears to the common eye with their poetic associations. Similarly, if we had *daughter* and *slaughter*, we were to write them *dochter* and *slauchter*, substituting in all cases *doon, froon, goon,* and *toon,* for *down, frown, gown,* and *town*. Then we made a list of Scottish idols, — pet words, national institutions, stock phrases, beloved objects, — convinced if we could weave them in we should attain 'atmosphere.' Here is the first list; it lengthened speedily: thistle, tartan, haar, haggis, kirk, claymore, parritch, broom, whin, sporran, whaup, plaid, scone, collops, whiskey, mutch, cairngorm, oatmeal, brae, kilt, brose, heather. Salemina and I were too devoted to common sense to succeed in this weaving process, so Penelope triumphed and won the first prize, both for that and also because she brought in a saying given us by Miss Dalziel, about the social classification of all Scotland into 'the gentlemen of the North, men of the South, people of the West, fowk o' Fife, and the Paisley bodies.' We think that her success came chiefly from her writing the verses with a Scotch plaid lead-pencil. What effect the absorption of so much red, blue, and green paint will have I cannot fancy, but she ate off — and up — all the tartan glaze before finishing the poem; it had a wonderfully stimulating effect, but the end is not yet!"

Of course there was a chorus of laughter when the young wretch exhibited my battered pencil, bought in Princes Street yesterday, its gay Gordon tints sadly disfigured by the destroying tooth, not of Time, but of a bard in the throes of composition.

"We bestowed a consolation prize on Salemina," continued Francesca, "because she succeeded in getting *hoots, losh, havers*, and *blathers* into one line, but naturally she could not maintain such an ideal standard. Read your verses, Pen, though there is little hope that our friends will enjoy them as much as you do. Whenever Miss Hamilton writes anything of this kind, she emulates her distinguished ancestor Sir William Hamilton, who always fell off his own chair in fits of laughter when he was composing verses."

With this inspiring introduction I read my lines as follows : —

AN AMERICAN LADY'S FAREWELL TO EDINBURGH

THE MUSE BEING SOMEWHAT UNDER THE INFLUENCE OF THE SCOTTISH BALLAD

I canna thole my ain toun,
Sin' I hae dwelt i' this;
To bide in Edinboro' reek,
Wad be the tap o' bliss.
Yon bonnie plaid aboot me hap,
The skirlin' pipes gae bring,
With thistles fair tie up my hair,
While I of Scotia sing.

The collops an' the cairngorms,
The haggis an' the whin,
The 'Stablished, Free, an' U. P. kirks,
The hairt convinced o' sin, —
The parritch an' the heather-bell,
The snawdrap on the shaw,
The bit lam's bleatin' on the braes, —
How can I leave them a'!

How can I leave the marmalade
An' bonnets o' Dundee?
The haar, the haddies, an' the brose,
The East win' blawin' free!
How can I lay my sporran by,
An' sit me doun at hame,
Wi'oot a Hieland philabeg
Or hyphenated name?

> I lo'e the gentry o' the North,
> The Southern men I lo'e,
> The canty people o' the West,
> The Paisley bodies too.
> The pawky fowk o' Fife are dear, —
> Sae dear are ane an' a',
> That e'en to think that we maun pairt
> Maist braks my hairt in twa.
>
> So fetch me tartans, heather, scones,
> An' dye my tresses red;
> I'd deck me like th' unconquer'd Scots
> Wha hae wi' Wallace bled.
> Then bind my claymore to my side,
> My kilt an' mutch gae bring;
> While Scottish lays soun' i' my lugs
> McKinley's no my king, —
>
> For Charlie, bonnie Stuart Prince,
> Has turned me Jacobite;
> I'd wear displayed the white cockade,
> An' (whiles) for him I'd fight!
> An' (whiles) I'd fight for a' that's Scotch,
> Save whuskey an' oatmeal,
> For wi' their ballads i' my bluid,
> Nae Scot could be mair leal!

I fancied that I had pitched my verses in so high a key that no one could mistake their burlesque intention. What was my confusion, however, to have one of the company remark when I finished, "Extremely pretty; but a mutch, you know, is an article of *woman's* apparel."

Mr. Macdonald flung himself gallantly into the breach. He is such a dear fellow! So quick, so discriminating, so warm-hearted!

"Don't pick flaws in Miss Hamilton's finest

line! That picture of a fair American, clad in a kilt and mutch, decked in heather and scones, and brandishing a claymore, will live forever in my memory. Don't clip the wings of her imagination! You will be telling her soon that one does n't tie one's hair with thistles, nor couple collops with cairngorms."

Somebody sent Francesca a great bunch of yellow broom, late that afternoon. There was no name in the box, she said, but at night she wore the odorous tips in the bosom of her black dinner-gown, and standing erect in her dark hair like golden aigrettes.

When she came into my room to say goodnight, she laid the pretty frock in one of my trunks, which was to be filled with the garments of fashionable society and left behind in Edinburgh. The next moment I chanced to look on the floor, and discovered a little card, a bent card, with two lines written on it:—

> "*Better lo'ed ye canna be,*
> *Will ye no come back again?*"

We have received many invitations in that handwriting. I know it well, and so does Francesca, though it is blurred; and the reason for this, according to my way of thinking, is that it has been lying next the moist stems of flowers, and, unless I do her wrong, very near to somebody's warm heart as well.

I will not betray her to Salemina, even to gain

a victory over that blind and deaf but much beloved woman. How could I, with my heart beating high at the thought of seeing my ain dear laddie before many days!

> "Oh, love, love, lassie,
> Love is like a dizziness:
> It winna let a puir body
> Gang aboot his business."

PART SECOND. IN THE COUNTRY

XIV

> " Now she 's cast aff her bonny shoon
>   Made o' gilded leather,
> And she 's put on her Hieland brogues
>   To skip amang the heather.
> And she 's cast aff her bonny goon
>   Made o' the silk and satin,
> And she 's put on a tartan plaid
>   To row amang the braken."
>
> *Lizzie Baillie.*

WE are in the East Neuk o' Fife; we are in Pettybaw; we are neither boarders nor lodgers; we are residents, inhabitants, householders, and we live (live, mind you) in a wee theekit hoosie in the old loaning. Words fail to tell you how absolutely Scotch we are and how blissfully happy. It is a happiness, I assure you, achieved through great tribulation. Salemina and I traveled many miles in railway trains, and many in various other sorts of wheeled vehicles, while the ideal ever beckoned us onward. I was determined to find a romantic lodging, Salemina a comfortable one, and this special combination of virtues is next to impossible, as every one knows. Linghurst was too much of a town; Bonnie Craig had no respectable inn; Whinnybrae was struggling to be a watering-place; Broomlea had no golf course within ten miles, and we intended to go back to our native land and win silver goblets in mixed foursomes; the "new toun o' Fairloch" (which looked centuries old) was delightful, but we could not find apartments there; Pinkie Leith was nice, but they were tearing up the "fore street" and laying drain-pipes in it. Strathdee had been highly recommended, but it rained when we were in Strathdee, and nobody can deliberately settle in a place where it rains during the process of deliberation. No train left this moist and dripping hamlet for three hours, so we took a covered trap and drove onward in melancholy mood. Suddenly the clouds lifted and the rain ceased; the driver thought we should be having settled weather now, and put back the top of the carriage, saying meanwhile that it was a verra dry simmer this year, and that the crops sairly needed shoo'rs.

"Of course, if there is any district in Scotland where for any reason droughts are possible, that is where we wish to settle," I whispered to Salemina; "though, so far as I can see, the Strathdee crops are up to their knees in mud. Here is another wee village. What is this place, driver?"

"Pettybaw, mam; a fine toun!"

"Will there be apartments to let there?"

"I couldna say, mam."

"Susanna Crum's father! How curious that he should live here!" I murmured; and at this moment the sun came out, and shone full, or at least almost full, on our future home.

"Pettybaw! *Petit bois*, I suppose," said Salemina; "and there, to be sure, it is, — the 'little wood' yonder."

We drove to the Pettybaw Inn and Posting Establishment, and, alighting, dismissed the driver. We had still three good hours of daylight, although it was five o'clock, and we refreshed ourselves with a delicious cup of tea before looking for lodgings. We consulted the greengrocer, the baker, and the flesher, about furnished apartments, and started on our quest, not regarding the little posting establishment as a possibility. Apartments we found to be very scarce, and in one or two places that were quite suitable the landlady refused to do any cooking. We wandered from house to house, the sun shining brighter and brighter, and Pettybaw looking lovelier and lovelier; and as we were refused shelter again and again, we grew more and more enamored, as is the manner of human kind. The blue sea sparkled, and Pettybaw Sands gleamed white a mile or two in the distance, the pretty stone church raised its carved spire from the green trees, the manse next door was hidden in vines, the sheep lay close to the gray stone walls and the young lambs nestled close beside them, while the song of the burn, tinkling merrily down the glade on the edge of which we stood, and the cawing of the rooks in the little wood, were the only sounds to be heard.

Salemina, under the influence of this sylvan solitude, nobly declared that she could and would do without a set bath-tub, and proposed building a cabin and living near to nature's heart.

"I think, on the whole, we should be more comfortable living near to the inn-keeper's heart," I answered. "Let us go back there and pass the night, trying thus the bed and breakfast, with a view to seeing what they are like,— though they did say in Edinburgh that nobody thinks of living in these wayside hostelries."

Back we went, accordingly, and after ordering dinner came out and strolled idly up the main street. A small sign in the draper's window, heretofore overlooked, caught our eye. " House and Garden To Let. Inquire Within." Inquiring within with all possible speed, we found the draper selling winseys, the draper's assistant tidying the ribbon-box, the draper's wife sewing in one corner, and the draper's baby playing on the clean floor. We were impressed favorably, and entered into negotiations without delay.

"The house will be in the loaning; do you mind, ma'am?" asked the draper. (We have long since discovered that this use of the verb is a bequest from the Gaelic, in which there is no present tense. Man never is, but always to be blessed, in that language, which in this particular is not unlike old-fashioned Calvinism.)

We went out of the back door and down the green loaning, until we came to the wee stone cottage in which the draper himself lives most of the year, retiring for the warmer months to the back of his shop, and eking out a comfortable income by renting his hearthstone to the summer visitor.

The thatched roof on the wing that formed the kitchen attracted my artist's eye, and we went in to examine the interior, which we found surprisingly attractive. There was a tiny sitting-room, with a fireplace and a microscopic piano; a dining-room adorned with portraits of relatives who looked nervous when they met my eye, for they knew that they would be turned face to the wall on the morrow; four bedrooms, a kitchen, and a back garden so filled with vegetables and flowers that we exclaimed with astonishment and admiration.

"But we cannot keep house in Scotland," objected Salemina. "Think of the care! And what about the servants?"

"Why not eat at the inn?" I suggested. "Think of living in a real loaning, Salemina! Look at the stone floor in the kitchen, and the adorable stuffy box-bed in the wall! Look at the bust of Sir Walter in the hall, and the chromo of Melrose Abbey by moonlight! Look at the lintel over the front door, with a ship, moon, stars, and 1602 carved in the stone! What is food to all this?"

Salemina agreed that it was hardly worth considering; and in truth so many landladies had refused to receive her as a·tenant that day, that her spirits were rather low, and she was uncommonly flexible.

"It is the lintel and the back garden that rents the hoose," remarked the draper complacently in broad Scotch that I cannot reproduce. He is a house-agent as well as a draper, and went on to tell us that when he had a cottage he could rent in no other way he planted plenty of creepers in front of it. "The baker's hoose is no sae bonnie," he said, "and the linen and cutlery verra scanty, but there is a yellow laburnum growin' by the door: the leddies see that, and forget to ask aboot the linen. It depends a good bit on the weather, too; it is easy to let a hoose when the sun shines upon it."

"We hardly dare undertake regular housekeeping," I said; "do your tenants ever take meals at the inn?"

"I couldna say, mam." (Dear, dear, the Crums are a large family!)

"If we did that, we should still need a servant to keep the house tidy," said Salemina, as we walked away. " Perhaps housemaids are to be had, though not nearer than Edinburgh, I fancy."

This gave me an idea, and I slipped over to the post-office while Salemina was preparing for dinner, and dispatched a telegram to Mrs. M'Collop at Breadalbane Terrace, asking her if she could send a reliable general servant to us, capable of cooking simple breakfasts and caring for a house.

We had scarcely finished our Scotch broth, fried haddies, mutton-chops, and rhubarb tart when I received an answer from Mrs. M'Collop to the effect that her sister's husband's niece, Jane Grieve, could join us on the morrow if desired. The relationship was an interesting fact, though we scarcely thought the information worth the additional threepence we paid for it in the telegram; however, Mrs. M'Collop's comfortable assurance, together with the quality of the rhubarb tart and mutton-chops, brought us to a decision. Before going to sleep we rented the draper's house, named it Bide-a-Wee Cottage, engaged daily luncheons and dinners for three persons at the Pettybaw Inn and Posting Establishment, telegraphed to Edinburgh for Jane Grieve, to Callender for Francesca, and dispatched a letter to Paris for Mr. Beresford, telling him we had taken a " wee theekit hoosie " and that the " yett was ajee " whenever he chose to come.

"Possibly it would have been wiser not to send for them until we were settled," I said reflectively. "Jane Grieve may not prove a suitable person."

"The name somehow sounds too young and inexperienced," observed Salemina, "and what association have I with the phrase 'sister's husband's niece'?"

"You have heard me quote Lewis Carroll's verse, perhaps:—

> 'He thought he saw a buffalo
> Upon the chimney-piece;
> He looked again and found it was
> His sister's husband's niece:
> "Unless you leave the house," he said,
> "I'll send for the police!"'

The only thing that troubles me," I went on, "is the question of Willie Beresford's place of residence. He expects to be somewhere within easy walking or cycling distance,— four or five miles at most."

"He won't be desolate even if he does n't have a thatched roof, a pansy garden, and a blossoming shrub," said Salemina sleepily, for our business arrangements and discussions had lasted well into the evening. "What he will want is a lodging where he can have frequent sight and speech of you. How I dread him! How I resent his sharing of you with us! I don't know why I use the word 'sharing,' forsooth! There is nothing half so fair and just in his majesty's greedy mind. Well, it's the way of the world; only it is odd, with the universe of women to choose from, that he must needs take you. Strathdee seems the most desirable place for him, if he has a mackintosh and rubber boots. Inchcaldy is another town near here that we did n't see at all, — that might do; the draper's wife says that we can send fine linen to the laundry there."

"Inchcaldy? Oh yes, I think we heard of it in Edinburgh — at least I have some association with the name: it has a fine golf course, I believe, and very likely we ought to have looked at it, though for my part I have no regrets. Nothing can equal Pettybaw; and I am so pleased to be a Scottish householder! Are n't we just like Bessie Bell and Mary Gray?

> 'They were twa bonnie lassies;
> They biggit a bower on yon burnbrae,
> An' theekit it ower wi' rashes.'

Think of our stone-floored kitchen, Salemina! Think of the real box-bed in the wall for little Jane Grieve! She will have red-gold hair, blue eyes, and a pink cotton gown. Think of our own cat! Think how Francesca will admire the 1602 lintel! Think of our back garden, with our own 'neeps' and vegetable marrows growing in it! Think how they will envy us at home when they learn that we have settled down into Scottish yeowomen!

> 'It's oh, for a patch of land!
> It's oh, for a patch of land!
> Of all the blessings tongue can name,
> There's nane like a patch of land!'

Think of Willie coming to step on the floor and look at the bed and stroke the cat and covet the lintel and walk in the garden and weed the turnips and pluck the marrows that grow by our ain wee theekit hoosie!"

"Penelope, you appear slightly intoxicated! Do close the window and come to bed."

"I am intoxicated with the caller air of Pettybaw," I rejoined, leaning on the window-sill and looking at the stars, while I thought: "Edinburgh was beautiful; it is the most beautiful gray city in the world; it lacked one thing only to make it perfect, and Pettybaw will have that before many moons.

> 'Oh, Willie's rare an' Willie's fair
> An' Willie's wondrous bonny;
> An' Willie's hecht to marry me
> Gin e'er he marries ony.
>
> 'O gentle wind that bloweth south,
> From where my love repaireth,
> Convey a word from his dear mouth,
> An' tell me how he fareth.'"

XV

> " Gae tak' awa' the china plates,
>   Gae tak' them far frae me;
> And bring to me a wooden dish,
>   It's that I'm best used wi'.
> And tak' awa' thae siller spoons
>   The like I ne'er did see,
> And bring to me the horn cutties,
>   They're good eneugh for me."
> *Earl Richard's Wedding.*

THE next day was one of the most cheerful and one of the most fatiguing that I ever spent. Salemina and I moved every article of furniture in our wee theekit hoosie from the place where it originally stood to another and a better place: arguing, of course, over the precise spot it should occupy, which was generally upstairs if the thing were already down, or downstairs if it were already up. We hid all the more hideous ornaments of the draper's wife, and folded away her most objectionable tidies and table-covers, replacing them with our own pretty draperies. There were only two pictures in the sitting-room, and as an artist I would not have parted with them for worlds. The first was The Life of a Fireman, which could only remind one of the explosion of a mammoth tomato, and the other was The Spirit of Poetry Calling Burns from the Plough. Burns wore white knee-breeches, military boots, a splendid waistcoat with lace ruffles, and carried a cocked hat. To have been so dressed he must have known the Spirit was intending to come. The plough-horse was a magnificent Arabian, whose tail swept the freshly furrowed earth, while the Spirit of Poetry was issuing from a practicable wigwam on the left, and was a lady of such ample dimensions that no poet would have dared say " no " when she called him.

The dining-room was blighted by framed photographs of the draper's relations and the draper's wife's relations; all uniformly ugly. (It seems strange that married couples having the least beauty to bequeath to their offspring should persist in having the largest families.) These ladies and gentlemen were too numerous to remove, so we obscured them with trailing branches; reflecting that we only breakfasted in the room, and the morning meal is easily digested when one lives in the open air. We arranged flowers everywhere, and bought potted plants at a little nursery hard by. We apportioned the bedrooms, giving Francesca the hardest bed, — as she is the youngest, and wasn't here to choose, — me the next hardest, and Salemina the best; Francesca the largest looking-glass and wardrobe, me the best view, and Salemina the biggest bath. We bought housekeeping stores, distributing our patronage equally between the two grocers; we purchased aprons and dusters from the rival drapers, engaged bread and rolls from the baker, milk and cream from the plumber, who keeps three cows, interviewed the flesher about chops; in fact, no young couple facing love in a cottage ever had a busier or happier time than we; and at sundown, when Francesca arrived, we were in the pink of order, standing under our own lintel, ready to welcome her to Pettybaw. As to being strangers in a strange land, we had a bowing acquaintance with everybody on the main street of the tiny village, and were on terms of considerable intimacy with half a dozen families, including dogs and babies.

Francesca was delighted with everything, from the station (Pettybaw Sands, two miles away) to Jane Grieve's name, which she thought as perfect, in its way, as Susanna Crum's. She had purchased a "tirling-pin," that old-time precursor of knockers and bells, at an antique shop in Oban, and we fastened it on the front door at once, taking turns at risping it until our own nerves were shattered, and the draper's wife ran down the loaning to see if we were in need of anything. The twisted bar of iron stands out from the door and the ring is drawn up and down over a series of nicks, making a rasping noise. The lovers and ghaists in the old ballads always "tirled at the pin," you remember; that is, touched it gently.

Francesca brought us letters from Edinburgh, and what was my joy, in opening Willie's, to learn that he begged us to find a place in Fifeshire, and as near St. Rules or Strathdee as convenient; for in that case he could accept an invitation he had just received to visit his friend Robin Anstruther, at Rowardennan Castle.

"It is not the visit at the castle I wish so much, you may be sure," he wrote, "as the fact that Lady Ardmore will make everything pleasant for you. You will like my friend Robin Anstruther, who is Lady Ardmore's youngest brother, and who is going to her to be nursed and coddled after a baddish accident in the hunting-field. He is very sweet-tempered, and will get on well with Francesca"—

"I don't see the connection," rudely interrupted that spirited young person.

"I suppose she has more room on her list in the country than she had in Edinburgh; but if my remembrance serves me, she always enrolls a goodly number of victims, whether she has any immediate use for them or not."

"Mr. Beresford's manners have not been improved by his residence in Paris," observed Francesca, with resentment in her tone and delight in her eye.

"Mr. Beresford's manners are always perfect,"

said Salemina loyally, " and I have no doubt that this visit to Lady Ardmore will be extremely pleasant for him, though very embarrassing to us. If we are thrown into forced intimacy with a castle" (Salemina spoke of it as if it had fangs and a lashing tail), "what shall we do in this draper's hut?"

"Salemina!" I expostulated, "the bears will devour you as they did the ungrateful child in the fairy-tale. I wonder at your daring to use the word 'hut' in connection with our wee theekit hoosie!"

"They will never understand that we are doing all this for the novelty of it," she objected. " The Scottish nobility and gentry probably never think of renting a house for a joke. Imagine Lord and Lady Ardmore, the young Ardmores, Robin Anstruther, and Willie Beresford calling upon us in this sitting-room! We ourselves would have to sit in the hall and talk in through the doorway."

"All will be well," Francesca assured her soothingly. "We shall be pardoned much because we are Americans, and will not be expected to know any better. Besides, the gifted Miss Hamilton is an artist, and that covers a multitude of sins against conventionality. When the castle people 'tirl at the pin,' I will appear as the maid, if you like, following your example at Mrs. Bobby's cottage in Belvern, Pen."

" And it is n't as if there were many houses to

choose from, Salemina, nor as if Bide-a-Wee Cottage were cheap," I continued. "Think of the rent we pay and keep your head high. Remember that the draper's wife says there is nothing half so comfortable in Inchcaldy, although that is twice as large a town."

"*Inchcaldy!*" ejaculated Francesca, sitting down heavily upon the sofa and staring at me.

"Inchcaldy, my dear, — spelled *caldy*, but pronounced *cawdy;* the town where you are to take your nonsensical little fripperies to be laundered."

"Where is Inchcaldy? How far away?"

"About five miles, I believe, but a lovely road."

"Well," she exclaimed bitterly, "of course Scotland is a small, insignificant country; but, tiny as it is, it presents some liberty of choice, and why you need have pitched upon Pettybaw, and brought me here, when it is only five miles from Inchcaldy, and a lovely road besides, is more than I can understand!"

"In what way has Inchcaldy been so unhappy as to offend you?" I asked.

"It has not offended me, save that it chances to be Ronald Macdonald's parish, — that is all."

"Ronald Macdonald's parish!" we repeated automatically.

"Certainly, — you must have heard him mention Inchcaldy; and how queer he will think it that I have come to Pettybaw, under all the circumstances!"

"We do not know 'all the circumstances,'" quoted Salemina somewhat haughtily; "and you must remember, my dear, that our opportunities for speech with Mr. Macdonald have been very rare when you were present. For my part, I was always in such a tremor of anxiety during his visits lest one or both of you should descend to blows that I remember no details of his conversation. Besides, we did not choose Pettybaw; we discovered it by chance as we were driving from Strathdee to St. Rules. How were we to know that it was near this fatal Inchcaldy? If you think it best, we will hold no communication with the place, and Mr. Macdonald need never know you are here."

I thought Francesca looked rather startled at this proposition. At all events she said hastily, "Oh well, let it go; we could not avoid each other long, anyway, though it is very awkward, of course; you see, we did not part friends."

"I thought I had never seen you on more cordial terms," remarked Salemina.

"But you were n't there," answered Francesca unguardedly.

"Were n't where?"

"Were n't there."

"Where?"

"At the station."

"What station?"

"The station in Edinburgh from which I started for the Highlands."

"You never said that he came to see you off."

"The matter was too unimportant for notice; and the more I think of his being here, the less I mind it, after all; and so, dull care, begone! When I first meet him on the sands or in the loaning, I shall say, 'Dear me, is it Mr. Macdonald! What brought you to our quiet hamlet?' (I shall put the responsibility on him, you know.) 'That is the worst of these small countries,— fowk are aye i' the gait! When we part forever in America, we are able to stay parted, if we wish.' Then he will say, 'Quite so, quite so; but I suppose even you, Miss Monroe, will allow that a minister may not move his church to please a lady.' 'Certainly not,' I shall reply, 'eespecially when it is Estaiblished!' Then he will laugh, and we shall be better friends for a few moments; and then I shall tell him my latest story about the Scotchman who prayed, 'Lord, I do not ask that Thou shouldst give me wealth; only show me where it is, and I will attend to the rest.'"

Salemina moaned at the delightful prospect opening before us, while I went to the piano and caroled impersonally:—

> "Oh, wherefore did I cross the Forth,
> And leave my love behind me?

>   Why did I venture to the north
>   With one that did not mind me?
>   I'm sure I've seen a better limb
>   And twenty better faces;
>   But still my mind it runs on him
>   When I am at the races!"

Francesca left the room at this, and closed the door behind her with such energy that the bust of Sir Walter rocked on the hall shelf. Running upstairs she locked herself in her bedroom, and came down again only to help us receive Jane Grieve, who arrived at eight o'clock.

In times of joy, Salemina, Francesca, and I occasionally have our trifling differences of opinion, but in hours of affliction we are as one flesh. An all-wise Providence sent us Jane Grieve for fear that we should be too happy in Pettybaw. Plans made in heaven for the discipline of sinful human flesh are always successful, and this was no exception.

We had sent a "machine" from the inn to meet her, and when it drew up at the door we went forward to greet the rosy little Jane of our fancy. An aged person, wearing a rusty black bonnet and shawl, and carrying what appeared to be a tin cake-box and a baby's bath-tub, descended rheumatically from the vehicle and announced herself as Miss Grieve. She was too old to call by her Christian name, too sensitive to call by her surname, so Miss Grieve she remained, as announced, to the end of the chapter, and our rosy little Jane died before she was actually born. The man took her curious luggage into the kitchen, and Salemina escorted her thither, while Francesca and I fell into each other's arms and laughed hysterically.

"Nobody need tell me that she is Mrs. M'Collop's sister's husband's niece," she whispered, "though she may possibly be somebody's grandaunt. Does n't she remind you of Mrs. Gummidge?"

Salemina returned in a quarter of an hour, and sank dejectedly on the sofa.

"Run over to the inn, Francesca," she said, "and order bacon and eggs at eight-thirty tomorrow morning. Miss Grieve thinks we had better not breakfast at home until she becomes accustomed to the surroundings."

"Shall we allow her to become accustomed to them?" I questioned.

"She came up from Glasgow to Edinburgh for the day, and went to see Mrs. M'Collop just as our telegram arrived. She was living with an 'extremely nice family' in Glasgow, and only broke her engagement in order to try Fifeshire air for the summer; so she will remain with us as long as she is benefited by the climate."

"Can't we pay her for a month and send her away?"

"How can we? She is Mrs. M'Collop's sister's husband's niece, and we intend returning to Mrs. M'Collop. She has a nice ladylike appearance, but when she takes her bonnet off she looks seventy years old."

"She ought always to keep it off, then," returned Francesca, "for she looked eighty with it on. We shall have to soothe her last moments, of course, and pay her funeral expenses. Did you offer her a cup of tea and show her the box-bed?"

"Yes; she said she was muckle obleeged to me, but the coals were so poor and hard she couldna batter them up to start a fire the nicht, and she would try the box-bed to see if she could sleep in it. I am glad to remember that it was you who telegraphed for her, Penelope."

"Let there be no recriminations," I responded; "let us stand shoulder to shoulder in this calamity,—isn't there a story called 'Calamity Jane?' We might live at the inn, and give her the cottage for a summer residence, but I utterly refuse to be parted from our cat and the 1602 lintel."

After I have once described Miss Grieve I shall not suffer her to begloom these pages as she did our young lives. She is so exactly like her kind in America that she cannot be looked upon as a national type. Everywhere we go we see fresh, fair-haired, sonsie lassies; why should we have been visited with this affliction, we who have no courage in a foreign land to rid ourselves of it?

She appears at the door of the kitchen with some complaint, and stands there talking to herself in a depressing murmur until she arrives at the next grievance. Whenever we hear this, which is whenever we are in the sitting-room, we amuse ourselves by chanting lines of melancholy poetry which correspond to the sentiments she seems to be uttering. It is the only way the infliction can be endured, for the sitting-room is so small we cannot keep the door closed habitually. The effect of this plan is something like the following : —

She. "The range has sic a bad draft I canna mak' the fire draw!"

We. "But I'm ower auld for the tears to start,
An' sae the sighs maun blaw!"

She. "The clock i' the hall doesna strike. I have to get oot o' my bed to see the time."

We. "The broken hairt it kens
Nae second spring again!"

She. "There are not eneuch jugs i' the hoose."

We. "I'm downright dizzy wi' the thought, —
In troth I'm like to greet!"

She. "The sink drain is na recht."

We. "An' it's oh! to win awa', awa',
An' it's oh! to win awa'!"

She. "I canna thole a box-bed!"

We. "Ay, waukin' O
Waukin' O an' weary.
Sleep I can get nane,
Ay waukin' O!"

She. "It's fair insultin' to rent a hoose wi' so few convenience."

We. "An' I'm ower auld to fish ony mair,
An' I hinna the chance to droon."

She. "The work is fair sickenin' i' this hoose, an' a' for ane puir body to do by her lane."

We. "How can ye chant, ye little birds,
An' I sae weary, fu' o' care?"

She. "Ah, but that was a fine family I lived wi' in Glasgy; an' it's a wearifu' day's work I've had the day."

We. "Oh, why was I spared to cry, wae's me!"

She. "Why dinna they leave floo'rs i' the garden, makin' sic a mess i' the hoose wi' 'em? It's not for the knowin' what they will be after next!"

We. "Oh, waly waly up the bank,
And waly waly doon the brae!"

Miss Grieve's plaints never grow less, though we are sometimes at a loss for appropriate quotations to match them. The poetic interpolations are introduced merely to show the general spirit of her conversation. They take the place of her sighs, which are by their nature unprintable. Many times each day she is wont to sink into one low chair, and, extending her feet in another, close her eyes and murmur undistinguishable plaints which come to us in a kind of rhythmic way. She has such a shaking right hand we have been obliged to give up coffee and have tea, as the former beverage became too unsettled on its journey from the kitchen to the breakfast-table. She says she kens she is a guid cook, though salf-praise is sma' racommendation (sma' as it is she will get no other!); but we have little opportunity to test her skill, as she prepares only our breakfasts of eggs and porridge. Visions of home-made goodies had danced before our eyes, but as the hall clock doesna strike she is unable to rise at any exact hour, and as the range draft is bad, and the coals too hard to batter up wi' a hatchet, we naturally have to content ourselves with the baker's loaf.

And this is a truthful portrait of " Calamity Jane," our one Pettybaw grievance.

XVI

> "Gae farer up the burn to Habbie's Howe,
>   Where a' the sweets o' spring an' simmer grow:
> Between twa birks, out o'er a little lin,
> The water fa's an' mak's a singan din;
> A pool breast-deep, beneath as clear as glass,
> Kisses, wi' easy whirls, the bord'ring grass."
>
> *The Gentle Shepherd.*

THAT is what Peggy says to Jenny in Allan Ramsay's poem, and if you substitute "Crummy-lowe" for "Habbie's Howe" in the first line, you will have a lovely picture of the Farm-Steadin'.

You come to it by turning the corner from the inn, first passing the cottage where the lady wishes to rent two rooms for fifteen shillings a week, but will not give much attendance, as she is slightly asthmatic, and the house is always as clean as it is this minute, and the view from the window looking out on Pettybaw Bay canna be surpassed at ony money. Then comes the little house where Will'am Beattie's sister Mary died in May, and there wasna a bonnier woman in Fife. Next is the cottage with the pansy garden, where the lady in the widow's cap takes five o'clock tea in the bay window, and a snug little supper at eight. She has for the first scones and marmalade, and her tea is in a small black teapot under a red cozy with a white muslin cover drawn over it. At eight she has more tea, and generally a kippered herring, or a bit of cold mutton left from the noon dinner. We note the changes in her bill of fare as we pass hastily by and feel admitted quite into the family secrets. Beyond this bay window, which is so redolent of simple peace and comfort that we long to go in and sit down, is the cottage with the double white tulips, the cottage with the collie on the front steps, the doctor's house with the yellow laburnum tree, and then the house where the Disagreeable Woman lives. She has a lovely baby, which, to begin with, is somewhat remarkable, as disagreeable women rarely have babies; or else, having had them, rapidly lose their disagreeableness, — so rapidly that one has not time to notice it. The Disagreeable Woman's house is at the end of the row, and across the road is a wicket gate leading — Where did it lead? — that was the very point. Along the left, as you lean wistfully over the gate, there runs a stone wall topped by a green hedge; and on the right, first furrows of pale fawn, then below, furrows of deeper brown, and mulberry, and red ploughed earth stretching down to waving fields of green, and thence to the sea, gray, misty, opalescent, melting into the pearly white clouds, so that one cannot tell where sea ends and sky begins.

There is a path between the green hedge and

the ploughed field, and it leads seductively to the farm-steadin'; or we felt that it might thus lead, if we dared unlatch the wicket gate. Seeing no sign "Private Way," "Trespassers Not Allowed," or other printed defiance to the stranger, we were considering the opening of the gate, when we observed two female figures coming toward us along the path, and paused until they should come through. It was the Disagreeable Woman (though we knew it not) and an elderly friend. We accosted the friend, feeling instinctively that she was framed of softer stuff, and asked her if the path were a private one. It was a question that had never met her ear before, and she was too dull or too discreet to deal with it on the instant. To our amazement, she did not even manage to falter, " I couldna say."

"Is the path private?" I repeated.

"It is certainly the idea to keep it a little private," said the Disagreeable Woman, coming into the conversation without being addressed. "Where do you wish to go?"

"Nowhere in particular. The walk looks so inviting we should like to see the end."

"It goes only to the Farm, and you can reach that by the highroad; it is only a half-mile farther. Do you wish to call at the Farm?"

"No, oh no; the path is so very pretty that"—

"Yes, I see; well, I should call it rather private." And with this she departed; leaving us to stand on the outskirts of paradise, while she went into her house and stared at us from the window as she played with the lovely undeserved baby. But that was not the end of the matter.

We found ourselves there next day, Francesca and I, — Salemina was too proud, — drawn by an insatiable longing to view the beloved and forbidden scene. We did not dare to glance at the Disagreeable Woman's windows, lest our courage should ooze away, so we opened the gate and stole through into the rather private path.

It was a most lovely path; even if it had not been in a sense prohibited, it would still have been lovely, simply on its own merits. There were little gaps in the hedge and the wall, through which we peered into a daisy-starred pasture, where a white bossy and a herd of flaxen-haired cows fed on the sweet green grass. The mellow ploughed earth on the right hand stretched down to the shore-line, and a ploughboy walked up and down the long, straight furrows whistling "My Nannie's awa'." Pettybaw is so far removed from the music-halls that their cheap songs and strident echoes never reach its sylvan shades, and the herd-laddies and ploughboys still sweeten their labors with the old classic melodies.

We walked on and on, determined to come every day; and we settled that if we were accosted by any one, or if our innocent business were demanded, Francesca should ask, " Does Mrs. Macstronachlacher live here, and has she any new-laid eggs?"

Soon the gates of the Farm appeared in sight. There was a cluster of buildings, with doves huddling and cooing on the red-tiled roofs, — dairy-houses, workmen's cottages, comely rows of haystacks (towering yellow things with peaked tops); a little pond with ducks and geese chattering together as they paddled about, and for additional music the trickling of two tiny burns making "a singan din" as they wimpled through the bushes. A speckle-breasted thrush perched on a corner of the gray wall and poured his heart out. Overhead there was a chorus of rooks in the tall trees, but there was no sound of human voice save that of the plough-laddie whistling " My Nannie's awa'."

We turned our backs on this darling solitude, and retraced our steps lingeringly. As we neared the wicket gate again we stood upon a bit of jutting rock and peered over the wall, sniffing the hawthorn buds with ecstasy. The white bossy drew closer, treading softly on its daisy carpet; the wondering cows looked up at us as they peacefully chewed their cuds; a man in corduroy breeches came from a corner of the pasture, and with a sharp, narrow hoe rooted out a thistle or two that had found their way into this sweet feeding-ground. Suddenly we heard the swish of a dress behind us, and turned, conscience-stricken, though we had in nothing sinned.

"Does Mrs. Macstronachlacher live here?" stammered Francesca like a parrot.

It was an idiotic time and place for the question. We had certainly arranged that she should ask it, but something must be left to the judgment in such cases. Francesca was hanging over a stone wall regarding a herd of cows in a pasture, and there was no possible shelter for a Mrs. Macstronachlacher within a quarter of a mile. What made the remark more unfortunate was the fact that, though she had on a different dress and bonnet, the person interrogated was the Disagreeable Woman; but Francesca is particularly slow in discerning resemblances. She would have gone on mechanically asking for new-laid eggs, had I not caught her eye and held it sternly. The foe looked at us suspiciously for a moment (Francesca's hats are not easily forgotten), and then vanished up the path, to tell the people at Crummylowe, I suppose, that their grounds were infested by marauding strangers whose curiosity was manifestly the outgrowth of a republican government.

As she disappeared in one direction, we

walked slowly in the other; and just as we reached the corner of the pasture where two stone walls meet, and where a group of oaks gives grateful shade, we heard children's voices.

"No, no!" cried somebody: "it must be still higher at this end, for the tower,—this is where the king will sit. Help me with this heavy one, Rafe. Dandie, mind your foot. Why don't you be making the flag for the ship?—and do keep the Wrig away from us till we finish building!"

XVII

"O lang, lang may the ladyes sit
   Wi' their face into their hand,
Before they see Sir Patrick Spens
   Come sailing to the strand."
                        Sir Patrick Spens.

WE forced our toes into the crevices of the wall and peeped stealthily over the top. Two boys of eight or ten years, with two younger children, were busily engaged in building a castle. A great pile of stones had been hauled to the spot, evidently for the purpose of mending the wall, and these were serving as rich material for sport. The oldest of the company, a bright-eyed, rosy-cheeked boy in an Eton jacket and broad white collar, was obviously commander-in-chief; and the next in size, whom he called Rafe, was a laddie of eight, in kilts. These two looked as if they might be scions of the aristocracy, while Dandie and the Wrig were fat little yokels of another sort. The miniature castle must have been the work of several mornings, and was worthy of the respectful but silent admiration with which we gazed upon it; but as the last stone was placed in the tower, the master builder looked up and spied our interested eyes peering at him over the wall. We were properly abashed and ducked our heads discreetly at once, but were reassured by hearing him run rapidly toward us, calling, "Stop, if you please! Have you anything on just now, — are you busy?"

We answered that we were quite at leisure.

"Then would you mind coming in to help us to play 'Sir Patrick Spens'? There are n't enough of us to do it nicely."

This confidence was touching, and luckily it was not in the least misplaced. Playing "Sir Patrick Spens" was exactly in our line, little as he suspected it.

"Come and help?" I said. "Simply delighted! Do come, Fanny dear. How can we get over the wall?"

"I'll show you the good broken place!" cried Sir Apple-Cheek; and following his directions we scrambled through, while Rafe took off his Highland bonnet ceremoniously and handed us down to earth.

"Hurrah! now it will be something like fun! Do you know 'Sir Patrick Spens'?"

"Every word of it. Don't you want us to pass an examination before you allow us in the game?"

"No," he answered gravely; "it's a great help, of course, to know it, but it is n't necessary. I keep the words in my pocket to prompt Dandie, and the Wrig can only say two lines, she's so little." (Here he produced some tattered leaves torn from a book of ballads.) "We've done it many a time, but this is a new Dunfermline Castle, and we are trying the play in a different way. Rafe is the king, and Dandie is the 'eldern knight,' — you remember him?"

"Certainly; he sat at the king's right knee."

"Yes, yes, that's the one! Then Rafe is Sir Patrick part of the time, and I the other part, because everybody likes to be him; but there's nobody left for the 'lords o' Noroway' or the sailors, and the Wrig is the only maiden to sit on the shore, and she always forgets to comb her hair and weep at the right time."

The forgetful and placid Wrig (I afterwards learned that this is a Scots word for the youngest bird in the nest) was seated on the grass, with her fat hands full of pink thyme and white wild woodruff. The sun shone on her curly flaxen head. She wore a dark blue cotton frock with white dots, and a short-sleeved pinafore; and though she was utterly useless from a dramatic point of view, she was the sweetest little Scotch dumpling I ever looked upon. She had been tried and found wanting in most of the principal parts of the ballad, but when left out of the performance altogether she was wont to scream so lustily that all Crummylowe rushed to her assistance.

"Now let us practice a bit to see if we know

what we are going to do," said Sir Apple-Cheek. "Rafe, you can be Sir Patrick this time. The reason why we all like to be Sir Patrick," he explained, turning to me, "is that the lords o' Noroway say to him, —

> 'Ye Scottishmen spend a' our King's gowd,
>   And a' our Queenis fee;'

and then he answers, —

> 'Ye lee! ye lee! ye leers loud,
>   Fu' loudly do ye lee!'

and a lot of splendid things like that. Well, I'll be the king," and accordingly he began: —

> "The King sits in Dunfermline tower,
>   Drinking the bluid-red wine.
> 'O whaur will I get a skeely skipper
>   To sail this new ship o' mine?'"

A dead silence ensued, whereupon the king said testily, "Now, Dandie, you never remember you're the eldern knight; go on!"

Thus reminded, Dandie recited: —

> "O up and spake an eldern knight
>   Sat at the King's right knee,
> 'Sir Patrick Spens is the best sailor
>   That ever sailed the sea.'"

"Now I'll write my letter," said the king, who was endeavoring to make himself comfortable in his somewhat contracted tower.

> "The King has written a braid letter
>   And sealed it with his hand;
> And sent it to Sir Patrick Spens,
>   Was walking on the strand.

Read the letter out loud, Rafe, and then you'll remember what to do."

> "'To Noroway! to Noroway!
> To Noroway on the faem!
> The King's daughter of Noroway,
> 'T is thou maun bring her hame,'"

read Rafe.

"Now do the next part!"

"I can't; I'm going to chuck up that next part. I wish you'd do Sir Pat until it comes to 'Ye lee! ye lee!'"

"No, that won't do, Rafe. We have to mix up everybody else, but it's too bad to spoil Sir Patrick."

"Well, I'll give him to you, then, and be the king. I don't mind so much now that we've got such a good tower; and why can't I stop up there even after the ship sets sail, and look out over the sea with a telescope? That's the way Elizabeth did the time she was king."

"You can stay till you have to come down and be a dead Scots lord. I'm not going to lie there as I did last time, with nobody but the Wrig for a Scots lord, and her forgetting to be dead!"

Sir Apple-Cheek then essayed the hard part "chucked up" by Rafe. It was rather difficult, I confess, as the first four lines were in pantomime and required great versatility: —

> "The first word that Sir Patrick read,
> Fu' loud, loud laughéd he;

> The neist word that Sir Patrick read,
> The tear blinded his e'e."

These conflicting emotions successfully simulated, Sir Patrick resumed:—

> "'O wha is he has dune this deed,
> And tauld the King o' me,—
> To send us out, at this time o' the year,
> To sail upon the sea?'"

Then the king stood up in the unstable tower and shouted his own orders:—

> "'Be it wind, be it weet, be it hail, be it sleet,
> Our ship maun sail the faem;
> The King's daughter o' Noroway,
> 'T is we maun fetch her hame.'"

"Can't we rig the ship a little better?" demanded our stage manager at this juncture. "It is n't half as good as the tower."

Ten minutes' hard work, in which we assisted, produced something a trifle more nautical and seaworthy than the first ship. The ground with a few boards spread upon it was the deck. Tarpaulin sheets were arranged on sticks to represent sails, and we located the vessel so cleverly that two slender trees shot out of the middle of it and served as the tall topmasts.

"Now let us make believe that we've hoisted our sails on 'Mononday morn' and been in Noroway 'weeks but only twae,'" said our leading man; "and your time has come now," turning to us.

We felt indeed that it had; but plucking up sufficient courage for the lords o' Noroway, we cried accusingly, —

> "'Ye Scottishmen spend a' our King's gowd,
>   And a' our Queenis fee!'"

Oh, but Sir Apple-Cheek was glorious as he roared virtuously: —

> "'Ye lee! ye lee! ye leers loud,
>   Fu' loudly do ye lee!
>
> 'For I brocht as much white monie
>   As gane my men and me,
> An' I brocht a half-fou o' gude red gowd
>   Out ower the sea wi' me.
>
> 'But betide me weil, betide me wae,
>   This day I'se leave the shore;
> And never spend my King's monie
>   'Mong Noroway dogs no more.
>
> 'Make ready, make ready, my merry men a',
>   Our gude ship sails the morn.'

Now you be the sailors, please!"

Glad to be anything but Noroway dogs, we recited obediently: —

> "'Now, ever alake, my master dear,
>   I fear a deadly storm!
>
> . . . . . .
>
> And if ye gang to sea, master,
>   I fear we'll come to harm.'"

We added much to the effect of this stanza by flinging ourselves on the turf and embracing Sir Patrick's knees, with which touch of melodrama he was enchanted.

Then came a storm so terrible that I can hardly trust myself to describe its fury. The entire *corps dramatique* personated the elements, and tore the gallant ship in twain, while Sir Patrick shouted in the teeth of the gale, —

> "'O whaur will I get a gude sailor
>   To tak' my helm in hand,
> Till I get up to the tall topmast
>   To see if I can spy land?'"

I knew the words a trifle better than Francesca, and thus succeeded in forestalling her as the fortunate hero : —

> "'O here am I, a sailor gude,
>   To tak' the helm in hand,
> Till you go up to the tall topmast;
>   But I fear ye 'll ne'er spy land.'"

And the heroic sailor was right, for

> "He hadna gone a step, a step,
>   A step but only ane,
> When a bout flew out o' our goodly ship,
>   And the saut sea it came in."

Then we fetched a web o' the silken claith, and anither o' the twine, as our captain bade us ; we wapped them into our ship's side and letna the sea come in ; but in vain, in vain. Laith were the gude Scots lords to weet their cork-heeled shune, but they did, and wat their hats abune ; for the ship sank in spite of their despairing efforts,

> "And mony was the gude lord's son
>   That never mair cam' hame."

Francesca and I were now obliged to creep from under the tarpaulins and personate the disheveled ladies on the strand.

"Will your hair come down?" asked the manager gravely.

"It will and shall," we rejoined; and it did.

> "The ladies wrang their fingers white,
> The maidens tore their hair."

"Do tear your hair, Jessie! It's the only thing you have to do, and you never do it on time!"

The Wrig made ready to howl with offended pride, but we soothed her, and she tore her yellow curls with her chubby hands.

> "And lang, lang may the maidens sit
> Wi' their gowd kaims i' their hair,
> A waitin' for their ain dear luves,
> For them they'll see nae mair."

I did a bit of sobbing here that would have been a credit to Sarah Siddons.

"Splendid! Grand!" cried Sir Patrick, as he stretched himself fifty fathoms below the imaginary surface, and gave explicit ante-mortem directions to the other Scots lords to spread themselves out in like manner.

> "Half ower, half ower to Aberdour,
> 'T is fifty fathoms deep,
> And there lies gude Sir Patrick Spens,
> Wi' the Scots lords at his feet."

"Oh, it is grand!" he repeated jubilantly.

"If I could only be the king and see it all from Dunfermline tower! Could you be Sir Patrick once, do you think, now that I have shown you how?" he asked Francesca.

"Indeed I could!" she replied, glowing with excitement (and small wonder) at being chosen for the principal rôle.

"The only trouble is that you do look awfully like a girl in that white frock."

Francesca appeared rather ashamed at her natural disqualifications for the part of Sir Patrick. "If I had only worn my long black cloak!" she sighed.

"Oh, I have an idea!" cried the boy. "Hand her the minister's gown from the hedge, Rafe. You see, Mistress Ogilvie of Crummylowe lent us this old gown for a sail; she's doing something to a new one, and this was her pattern."

Francesca slipped it on over her white serge, and the Pettybaw parson should have seen her with the long veil of her dark locks floating over his ministerial garment.

"It seems a pity to put up your hair," said the stage manager critically, "because you look so jolly and wild with it down, but I suppose you must; and will you have Rafe's bonnet?"

Yes, she would have Rafe's bonnet; and when she perched it on the side of her head and paced the deck restlessly, while the black gown floated behind in the breeze, we all cheered with enthusiasm, and, having rebuilt the ship, began the play again from the moment of the gale. The wreck was more horribly realistic than ever, this time, because of our rehearsal; and when I crawled from under the masts and sails to seat myself on the beach with the Wrig, I had scarcely strength enough to remove the cooky from her hand and set her a-combing her curly locks.

When our new Sir Patrick stretched herself on the ocean bed, she fell with a despairing wail; her gown spread like a pall over the earth, the Highland bonnet came off, and her hair floated over a haphazard pillow of Jessie's wild flowers.

"Oh, it is fine, that part; but from here is where it always goes wrong!" cried the king from the castle tower. "It's too bad to take the maidens away from the strand where they look so bonnie, and Rafe is splendid as the gude sailor, but Dandie looks so silly as one little dead Scots lord; if we only had one more person, young or old, if he was ever so stupid!"

"*Would I do?*"

This unexpected offer came from behind one of the trees that served as topmasts, and at the same moment there issued from that delightfully secluded retreat Ronald Macdonald, in knickerbockers and a golf cap.

Suddenly as this apparition came, there was no lack of welcome on the children's part. They shouted his name in glee, embraced his legs, and pulled him about like affectionate young bears. Confusion reigned for a moment, while Sir Patrick rose from her sea grave all in a mist of floating hair, from which hung impromptu garlands of pink thyme and green grasses.

"Allow me to do the honors, please, Jamie," said Mr. Macdonald, when he could escape from the children's clutches. "Have you been properly presented? I suppose not. Ladies, the young Master of Rowardennan. Jamie, Miss Hamilton and Miss Monroe from the United States of America." Sir Apple-Cheek bowed respectfully. "Let me present the Honorable Ralph Ardmore, also from the castle, together with Dandie Dinmont and the Wrig from Crummylowe. Sir Patrick, it is indeed a pleasure to see you again. Must you take off my gown? I had thought it was past use, but it never looked so well before."

"*Your* gown?"

The counterfeit presentment of Sir Patrick vanished as the long drapery flew to the hedge whence it came, and there remained only an offended young goddess, who swung her dark mane tempestuously to one side, plaited it in a thick braid, tossed it back again over her white serge shoulder, and crowded on her sailor hat with unnecessary vehemence.

"Yes, *my* gown; whose else could you more appropriately borrow, pray? Mistress Ogilvie of

Crummylowe presses, sponges, and darns my bachelor wardrobe, but I confess I never suspected that she rented it out for theatrical purposes. I have been calling upon you in Pettybaw; Lady Ardmore was there at the same time. Finding but one of the three American Graces at home, I stayed a few moments only, and am now returning to Inchcaldy by way of Crummylowe." Here he plucked the gown off the hedge and folded it carefully.

"Can't we keep it for a sail, Mr. Macdonald?" pleaded Jamie. "Mistress Ogilvie said it was n't any more good."

"When Mistress Ogilvie made that remark," replied the Reverend Ronald, "she had no idea that it would ever touch the shoulders of the martyred Sir Patrick Spens. Now I happen to love" —

Francesca hung out a scarlet flag in each cheek, and I was about to say, "Don't mind me!" when he continued: —

"As I was saying, I happen to love 'Sir Patrick Spens,' — it is my favorite ballad; so, with your permission, I will take the gown, and you can find something less valuable for a sail!"

I could never understand just why Francesca was so annoyed at being discovered in our innocent game. Of course she was prone on Mother Earth and her tresses were much disheveled, but she looked lovely, after all, in comparison with me, the humble " supe " and lightning-change artist; yet I kept my temper, — at least I kept it until the Reverend Ronald observed, after escorting us through the gap in the wall, " By the way, Miss Hamilton, there was a gentleman from Paris at your cottage, and he is walking down the road to meet you."

Walking down the road to meet me, forsooth! Have ministers no brains? The Reverend Mr. Macdonald had wasted five good minutes with his observations, introductions, explanations, felicitations, and adorations, and meantime, regardez-moi, messieurs et mesdames, s'il vous plait! I have been a Noroway dog, a ship-builder, and a gallant sailorman; I have been a gurly sea and a towering gale; I have crawled from beneath broken anchors, topsails, and mizzenmasts to a strand where I have been a suffering lady plying a gowd kaim. My skirt of blue drill has been twisted about my person until it trails in front; my collar is wilted, my cravat untied; I have lost a stud and a sleeve-link; my hair is in a tangled mass, my face is scarlet and dusty — and a gentleman from Paris is walking down the road to meet me!

XVIII

> "There were three ladies in a hall —
> With a heigh-ho! and a lily gay,
> There came a lord among them all —
> As the primrose spreads so sweetly."
> *The Cruel Brother.*

WILLIE BERESFORD has come to Pettybaw, and that Arcadian village has received the last touch that makes it Paradise.

We are exploring the neighborhood together, and whichever path we take we think it lovelier than the one before. This morning we drove to Pettybaw Sands, Francesca and Salemina following by the footpath and meeting us on the shore. It is all so enchantingly fresh and green on one of these rare bright days : the trig lass bleaching her " claes " on the grass by the burn near the little stone bridge ; the wild partridges whirring about in pairs ; the farm-boy seated on the clean straw in the bottom of his cart, and cracking his whip in mere wanton joy at the sunshine ; the pretty cottages, and the gardens with rows of currant and gooseberry bushes hanging thick with fruit that suggests jam and tart in every delicious globule. It is a love-colored landscape, we know it full well ; and nothing in the fair world about us is half as beautiful as what we see in each other's eyes. Ah, the memories of these first golden mornings together after our long separation. I shall sprinkle them with lavender and lay them away in that dim chamber of the heart where we keep precious things. We all know the chamber. It is fragrant with other hidden treasures, for all of them are sweet, though some are sad. This is the reason why we put a finger on the lip and say "Hush," if we open the door and allow any one to peep in.

We tied the pony by the wayside and alighted: Willie to gather some sprays of the pink veronica and blue speedwell, I to sit on an old bench and watch him in happy idleness. The "white-blossomed slaes" sweetened the air, and the distant hills were gay with golden whin and broom, or flushed with the purply-red of the bell heather.

We heard the note of the cushats from a neighboring bush. They used to build their nests on the ground, so the story goes, but the cows trampled them. Now they are wiser and build higher, and their cry is supposed to be a derisive one, directed to their ancient enemies, "Come noo, Coo, Coo! Come noo!"

A hedgehog crept stealthily along the ground, and at a sudden sound curled himself up like a wee brown bear. There were women working in the fields near by, — a strange sight to our eyes at first, but nothing unusual here, where many of them are employed on the farms all the year round, sowing, weeding, planting, even ploughing in the spring, and in winter working at threshing or in the granary.

An old man, leaning on his staff, came tottering feebly along, and sank down on the bench beside me. He was dirty, ragged, unkempt, and feeble, but quite sober, and pathetically anxious for human sympathy.

"I'm achty-sax year auld," he maundered, apropos of nothing, "achty-sax year auld. I've seen five lairds o' Pettybaw, sax placed meenisters, an' seeven doctors. I was a mason an' a stoot mon i' thae days, but it's a meeserable life now. Wife deid, bairns deid! I sit by my lane, an' smoke my pipe, wi' naebody to gi'e me a sup o' water. Achty-sax is ower auld for a mon, — ower auld."

These are the sharp contrasts of life one cannot bear to face when one is young and happy. Willie gave him a half-crown and some tobacco for his pipe, and when the pony trotted off briskly, and we left the shrunken figure alone on his bench as he was lonely in his life, we kissed each other and pledged ourselves to look after him as long as we remain in Pettybaw; for what is love worth if it does not kindle the flames of spirit, open the gates of feeling, and widen the heart to shelter all the little loves and great loves that crave admittance?

As we neared the tiny fishing-village on the sands we met a fishwife brave in her short skirt and eight petticoats, the basket with its two hundred pound weight on her head, and the auld wife herself knitting placidly as she walked along. They look superbly strong, these women; but, to be sure, the "weak anes dee," as one of them told me.

There was an air of bustle about the little quay, —

> "That joyfu' din when the boats come in,
> When the boats come in sae early;
> When the lift is blue an' the herring-nets fu',
> And the sun glints in a' things rarely."

The silvery shoals of fish no longer come so near the shore as they used in the olden time, for then the kirk bell of St. Monan's had its tongue tied when the "draive" was off the coast, lest its knell should frighten away the shining myriads of the deep.

We climbed the shoulder of a great green cliff until we could sit on the rugged rocks at the top and overlook the sea. The bluff is well named Nirly Scaur, and a wild, desolate spot it is, with gray lichen-clad boulders and stunted heather on its summit. In a storm here, the wind buffets and slashes and scourges one like invisible whips, and below, the sea churns itself into foaming waves, driving its " infinite squadrons of wild white horses " eternally toward the shore. It was calm and blue to-day, and no sound disturbed the quiet save the incessant shriek and scream of the rock birds, the kittiwakes, black-headed gulls, and guillemots that live on the sides of these high, sheer craigs. Here the mother guillemot lays her single egg, and here, on these narrow shelves of precipitous rock, she holds it in place with her foot until the warmth of her leg and overhanging body hatches it into life, when she takes it on her back and flies down to the sea. Motherhood under difficulties, it would seem, and the education of the baby guillemot is carried forward on Spartan principles; for the moment he is out of the shell he is swept downward hundreds of feet and plunged into a cold ocean, where he can sink or swim as instinct serves him. In a life so fraught with anxieties, exposures, and dangers, it is not strange that the guillemots keep up a ceaseless clang of excited conversation, a very riot and wrangle of altercation and argument which the circumstances seem to warrant. The prospective father is obliged to take turns with the prospective mother and hold the one precious egg on the rock while she goes for a fly, a swim, a bite, and a sup. As there are five hundred other parents on the same rock, and the eggs look to be only a couple of inches apart, the scene must be distracting, and I have no doubt we should find, if statistics were gathered, that thousands of guillemots die of nervous prostration.

Willie and I interpreted the clamor somewhat as follows : —

[*Between parent birds.*]

"I am going to take my foot off. Are you ready to put yours on? Don't be clumsy! Wait a minute, I'm not ready. *I'm not ready, I tell you!* NOW!!"

[*Between rival mothers.*]

"Your egg is so close to mine that I can't breathe" —

"Move your egg, then, I can't move mine!"

"You're sitting so close, I can't stretch my wings."

"Neither can I. You've got as much room as I have."

"I shall tumble if you crowd me."

"Go ahead and tumble, then! There is plenty of room in the sea."

[*From one father to another, ceremoniously.*]

"Pardon me, but I am afraid I shoved your wife off the rock last night."

"Don't mention it. I remember I shoved off your wife's mother last year."

We walked among the tiny whitewashed low-roofed cots, each with its silver-skinned fishes tacked invitingly against the door-frame to dry, until we came to my favorite, the corner cottage in the row. It has beautiful narrow garden strips in front, — solid patches of color in sweet gilly-flower bushes, from which the kindly housewife plucked a nosegay for us. Her white columbines she calls "granny's mutches;" and indeed they are not unlike those fresh white caps. Dear Robbie Burns, ten inches high in plaster, stands in the sunny window in a tiny box of blossoming plants surrounded by a miniature green picket fence. Outside, looming white among the gillyflowers, is Sir Walter, and near him is still another and a larger bust on a cracked pedestal a foot high, perhaps. We did not recognize the head at once, and asked the little woman who it was.

"Homer, the graund Greek poet," she answered cheerily; "an' I'm to have anither o' Burns, as tall as Homer, when my daughter comes hame frae E'nbro'."

If the shade of Homer keeps account of his earthly triumphs, I think he is proud of his place in that humble Scotchwoman's gillyflower garden, with his head under the drooping petals of granny's white mutches.

What do you think her "mon" is called in the village? John o' Mary! But he is not alone in his meekness, for there are Jock o' Meg, Willie o' Janet, Jem o' Tibby, and a dozen others. These primitive fishing-villages are the places where all the advanced women ought to congregate, for the wife is head of the house; the accountant, the treasurer, the auditor, the chancellor of the exchequer; and though her husband does catch the fish for her to sell, that is accounted apparently as a detail too trivial for notice.

When we passed Mary's cottage, on our way to the sands next day, Burns's head had been accidentally broken off by the children, and we felt as though we had lost a friend; but Scotch thrift, and loyalty to the dear Ploughman Poet, came to the rescue, and when we returned, Robbie's plaster head had been glued to his body. He smiled at us again from between the two scarlet geraniums, and a tendril of ivy had been gently curled about his neck to hide the cruel wound.

After such long, lovely mornings as this, there is a late luncheon under the shadow of a rock with Salemina and Francesca, an idle chat, or the chapter of a book, and presently Lady Ardmore and her daughter Elizabeth drive down to the sands. They are followed by Robin Anstruther, Jamie, and Ralph on bicycles, and before long the stalwart figure of Ronald Macdonald appears in the distance, just in time for a cup of tea, which we brew in Lady Ardmore's bath-house on the beach.

XIX

> " To you I sing, in simple Scottish lays,
>   The lowly train in life's sequester'd scene ;
>   The native feelings strong, the guileless ways."
> *The Cotter's Saturday Night.*

WE have lived in Pettybaw a very short time, but I see that we have already made an impression upon all grades of society. This was not our intention. We gave Edinburgh as our last place of residence, with the view of concealing our nationality, until such time as we should choose to declare it ; that is, when public excitement with regard to our rental of the house in the loaning should have lapsed into a state of indifference. And yet, modest, economical, and commonplace as has been the administration of our affairs, our method of life has evidently been thought unusual, and our conduct not precisely the conduct of other summer visitors. Even our daily purchases, in manner, in number, and in character, seem to be looked upon as eccentric, for whenever we leave a shop, the relatives of the greengrocer, flesher, draper, whoever it may be, bound downstairs, surround him in an eager circle, and inquire the latest news.

In an unwise moment we begged the draper's

wife to honor us with a visit and explain the obliquities of the kitchen range and the tortuosities of the sink-spout to Miss Grieve. While our landlady was on the premises, I took occasion to invite her up to my own room, with a view of seeing whether my mattress of pebbles and iron-filings could be supplemented by another of shavings or straw, or some material less provocative of bodily injuries. She was most sympathetic, persuasive, logical, and after the manner of her kind proved to me conclusively that the trouble lay with the too-saft occupant of the bed, not with the bed itself, and gave me statistics with regard to the latter which established its reputation and at the same moment destroyed my own.

She looked in at the various doors casually as she passed up and down the stairs, — all save that of the dining-room, which Francesca had prudently locked to conceal the fact that we had covered the family portraits, — and I noticed at the time that her face wore an expression of mingled grief and astonishment. It seemed to us afterward that there was a good deal more passing up and down the loaning than when we first arrived. At dusk especially, small processions of children and young people walked by our cottage and gave shy glances at the windows.

Finding Miss Grieve in an unusually amiable mood, I inquired the probable cause of this phenomenon. She would not go so far as to give any judicial opinion, but offered a few conjectures.

It might be the tirling-pin; it might be the white satin ribbons on the curtains; it might be the guitars and banjos; it might be the bicycle crate; it might be the profusion of plants; it might be the continual feasting and revelry; it might be the blazing fires in a Pettybaw summer. She thought a much more likely reason, however, was because it had become known in the village that we had moved every stick of furniture in the house out of its accustomed place and taken the dressing-tables away from the windows, — "thae windys," she called them.

I discussed this matter fully with Mr. Anstruther later on. He laughed heartily, but confessed, with an amused relish of his national conservatism, that to his mind there certainly was something radical, advanced, and courageous in taking a dressing-table away from its place, back to the window, and putting it anywhere else in a room. He would be frank, he said, and acknowledge that it suggested an undisciplined and lawless habit of thought, a disregard for authority, a lack of reverence for tradition, and a riotous and unbridled imagination.

This view of the matter gave us exquisite enjoyment. "But why?" I asked laughingly. "The dressing-table is not a sacred object, even to a woman. Why treat it with such veneration?

Where there is but one good light, and that immediately in front of the window, there is every excuse for the British custom, but when the light is well diffused, why not place the table wherever it looks well?"

"Ah, but it does n't look well anywhere but back to the window," said Mr. Anstruther artlessly. "It belongs there, you see; it has probably been there since the time of Malcolm Canmore, unless Margaret was too pious to look in a mirror. With your national love of change, you cannot conceive how soothing it is to know that whenever you enter your gate and glance upward, you will always see the curtains parted, and between them, like an idol in a shrine, the ugly wooden back of a little oval or oblong looking-glass. It gives one a sense of permanence in a world where all is fleeting."

The public interest in our doings seems to be entirely of a friendly nature, and if our neighbors find a hundredth part of the charm and novelty in us that we find in them, they are fortunate indeed, and we cheerfully sacrifice our privacy on the altar of the public good.

A village in Scotland is the only place I can fancy where housekeeping becomes an enthralling occupation. All drudgery disappears in a rosy glow of unexpected, unique, and stimulating conditions. I would rather superintend Miss Grieve and cause the light of amazement to gleam ten times daily in her humid eye, than lead a cotillion with Willie Beresford. I would rather do the marketing for our humble breakfasts and teas, or talk over the day's luncheons and dinners with Mistress Brodie of the Pettybaw Inn and Posting Establishment, than go to the opera.

Salemina and Francesca do not enjoy it all quite as intensely as I, so they considerately give me the lion's share. Every morning, after an exhilarating interview with the Niobe of our kitchen (who thinks me irresponsible and prays Heaven in her heart I be no worse), I put on my galoshes, take my umbrella, and trudge up and down the little streets and lanes on real, and if need be, imaginary errands. The Duke of Wellington said, "When fair in Scotland, always carry an umbrella; when it rains, please yourself," and I sometimes agree with Stevenson's shivering statement, "Life does not seem to me to be an amusement adapted to this climate." I quoted this to the doctor yesterday, but he remarked with some surprise that he had not missed a day's golfing for weeks. The chemist observed as he handed me a cake of soap, "Won-'erful blest in weather, we are, mam," simply because, the rain being unaccompanied with high wind, one was enabled to hold up an umbrella without having it turned inside out. When it ceased dripping for an hour at noon, the greengrocer said cheerily, "Another grand day, mam!" I assented, though I could not for the life of me remember when the last one occurred. However, dreary as the weather may be, one cannot be dull when doing one's morning round of shopping in Pettybaw or Strathdee. I have only to give you thumb-nail sketches of our favorite tradespeople to convince you of that fact.

. . . .

We bought our first groceries of Mrs. Robert Phin, of Strathdee, simply because she is an inimitable conversationalist. She is expansive, too, about family matters, and tells us certain of her "mon's" faults which it would be more seemly to keep in the safe shelter of her own bosom.

Rab takes a wee drappie too much, it appears, and takes it so often that he has little time to earn an honest penny for his family. This is bad enough; but the fact that Mrs. Phin has been twice wed before, and that in each case she innocently chose a ne'er-do-weel for a mate, makes her a trifle cynical. She told me that she had laid twa husbands in the kirkyard near which her little shop stands, and added cheerfully, as I made some sympathetic response, "An' I hope it'll no be lang afore I box Rab!"

Salemina objects to the shop because it is so disorderly. Soap and sugar, tea and bloaters, starch and gingham, lead pencils and sausages, lie side by side cosily. Boxes of pins are kept on top of kegs of herrings. Tins of coffee are distributed impartially anywhere and everywhere, and the bacon sometimes reposes in a glass case with small wares and findings, out of the reach of Alexander's dogs.

Alexander is one of a brood, or perhaps I should say three broods, of children which wander among the barrels and boxes and hams and winseys seeking what they may devour, — a handful of sugar, a prune, or a sweetie.

We often see the bairns at their luncheon or dinner in a little room just off the shop, Alexander the Small always sitting or kneeling on a "creepie," holding his plate down firmly with the left hand and eating with the right, whether the food be fish, porridge, or broth. In the Phin family the person who does not hold his plate down runs the risk of losing it to one of the other children or to the dogs, who, with eager eye and reminding paw, gather round the hospitable board, licking their chops hopefully.

I enjoy these scenes very much, but alas, I can no longer witness them as often as formerly.

This morning Mrs. Phin greeted me with some embarrassment.

"Maybe ye'll no ken me," she said, her usually clear speech a little blurred. "It's the teeth. I've mislaid 'em somewhere. I paid far too much siller for 'em to wear 'em ilka day. Sometimes I rest 'em in the tea-box to keep 'em awa' frae the bairns, but I canna find 'em theer. I'm thinkin' maybe they'll be in the rice, but I've been ower thrang to luik!"

This anecdote was too rich to keep to myself, but its unconscious humor made no impression upon Salemina, who insisted upon the withdrawal of our patronage. I have tried to persuade her that, whatever may be said of tea and rice, we run no risk in buying eggs; but she is relentless.

. . . .

The kirkyard where Rab's two predecessors have been laid, and where Rab will lie when Mrs. Phin has "boxed" him, is a sleepy little place set on a gentle slope of ground, softly shaded by willow and yew trees. It is inclosed by a stone wall, into which an occasional ancient tombstone is built, its name and date almost obliterated by stress of time and weather.

We often walk through its quiet, myrtle-bordered paths on our way to the other end of the village, where Mrs. Bruce, the flesher, keeps an unrivaled assortment of beef and mutton. The headstones, many of them laid flat upon the graves, are interesting to us because of their quaint inscriptions, in which the occupation of the deceased is often stated with modest pride and candor. One expects to see the achievements of the soldier, the sailor, or the statesman carved in the stone that marks his resting-place, but to our eyes it is strange enough to read that the subject of eulogy was a plumber, tobacconist, maker of golf-balls, or a golf champion; in which latter case there is a spirited etching or bas-relief of the dead hero, with knickerbockers, cap, and clubs complete.

There, too, lies Thomas Loughead, Hairdresser, a profession far too little celebrated in song and story. His stone is a simple one and bears merely the touching tribute: —

He was lovely and pleasant in his life,

the inference being to one who knows a line of Scripture, that in his death he was not divided.

These kirkyard personalities almost lead one to believe in the authenticity of the British tradesman's epitaph, wherein his practical-minded relict stated that the "bereaved widow would continue to carry on the tripe and trotter business at the old stand."

. . . .

One day when we were walking through the little village of Strathdee we turned the corner of a quiet side street and came suddenly upon something altogether strange and unexpected.

A stone cottage of the every-day sort stood a little back from the road and bore over its front door a sign announcing that Mrs. Bruce, Flesher, carried on her business within; and indeed one could look through the windows and see ruddy joints hanging from beams, and piles of pink and white steaks and chops lying neatly on the counter, crying, "Come, eat me!" Nevertheless, one's first glance would be arrested neither by Mrs. Bruce's black-and-gold sign, nor by the enticements of her stock in trade, because one's attention is knocked squarely between the eyes by an astonishing shape that arises from the patch of lawn in front of the cottage, and completely dominates the scene. Imagine yourself face to face with the last thing you would expect to see in a modest front dooryard, — the figurehead of a ship, heroic in size, gorgeous in color, majestic in pose! A female personage it appears to be from the drapery, which is the only key the artist furnishes as to sex, and a queenly female withal, for she wears a crown at least a foot high, and brandishes a forbidding sceptre. All this is seen from the front, but the rear view discloses the fact that the lady terminates in the tail of a fish which wriggles artistically in mid-air and is of a brittle sort, as it has evidently been thrice broken and glued together.

Mrs. Bruce did not leave us long in suspense, but obligingly came out, partly to comment on the low price of mutton and partly to tell the tale of the mammoth mermaid. By rights, of course, Mrs. Bruce's husband should have been the gallant captain of a bark which foundered at sea and sent every man to his grave on the ocean bed. The ship's figurehead should have been discovered by some miracle, brought to the sorrowing widow, and set up in the garden in eternal remembrance of the dear departed. This was the story in my mind, but as a matter of fact the rude effigy was wrought by Mrs. Bruce's father for a ship to be called the Sea Queen, but by some mischance, ship and figurehead never came together, and the old wood-carver left it to his daughter, in lieu of other property. It has not been wholly unproductive, Mrs. Bruce fancies, for the casual passers-by, like those who came to scoff and remained to pray, go into the shop to ask questions about the Sea Queen and buy chops out of courtesy and gratitude.

. . . .

On our way to the bakery, which is a daily walk with us, we always glance at a little cot in a grassy lane just off the fore street. In one half of this humble dwelling Mrs. Davidson keeps a slender stock of shop-worn articles, — pins, needles, threads, sealing-wax, pencils, and sweeties for the children, all disposed attractively upon a single shelf behind the window.

Across the passage, close to the other window, sits day after day an old woman of eighty-six summers who has lost her kinship with the present and gone back to dwell forever in the past. A small table stands in front of her rush-bottomed chair, the old family Bible rests on it, and in front of the Bible are always four tiny dolls, with which the trembling old fingers play from morning till night. They are cheap, common little puppets, but she robes and disrobes them with tenderest care. They are put to bed upon the Bible, take their walks along its time-worn pages, are married on it, buried on it, and the direst punishment they ever receive is to be removed from its sacred covers and temporarily hidden beneath the dear old soul's black alpaca apron. She is quite happy with her treasures on week days; but on Sundays — alas and alas! the poor old dame sits in her lonely chair with the furtive tears dropping on her wrinkled cheeks, for it is a God-fearing household, and it is neither lawful nor seemly to play with dolls on the Sawbath!

. . . .

Mrs. Nicolson is the presiding genius of the bakery; she is more — she is the bakery itself. A Mr. Nicolson there is, and he is known to be the baker, but he dwells in the regions below the shop and only issues at rare intervals, beneath the friendly shelter of a huge tin tray filled with scones and baps.

If you saw Mrs. Nicolson's kitchen with the firelight gleaming on its bright copper, its polished candlesticks, and its snowy floor, you would think her an admirable housewife, but you would get no clue to those shrewd and masterful traits of character which reveal themselves chiefly behind the counter.

Miss Grieve had purchased of Mrs. Nicolson a quarter section of very appetizing ginger cake to eat with our afternoon tea, and I stopped in to buy more. She showed me a large, round loaf for two shillings.

"No," I objected, "I cannot use a whole loaf, thank you. We eat very little at a time and like it perfectly fresh. I wish a small piece such as my maid bought the other day."

Then ensued a discourse which I cannot render in the vernacular, more's the pity, though I understood it all too well for my comfort. The substance of it was this: that she couldna and wouldna tak' it in hand to give me a quarter section of cake when the other three quarters might gae dry in the bakery; that the reason she sold the small piece on the former occasion was that her daughter, her son-in-law, and their three children came from Ballahoolish to visit her, and she gave them a high tea with no expense spared; that at this function they devoured three fourths of a ginger cake, and just as she was mournfully regarding the remainder my servant came in and took it off her hands; that she had kept a bakery for thirty years and her mother before her, and never had a two-shilling ginger cake been sold in pieces before, nor was it likely ever to occur again; that if I, under Providence so to speak, had been the fortunate gainer by the transaction, why not eat my six-pennyworth in solemn gratitude once for all, and not expect a like miracle to happen the next week? And finally, that two-shilling ginger cakes were, in the very nature of things, designed for large families; and it was the part of wisdom for small families to fix their affections on something else, for she couldna and wouldna tak' it in hand to cut a rare and expensive article for a small customer.

The torrent of logic was over, and I said humbly that I would take the whole loaf.

"Verra weel, mam," she responded more affably, "thank you kindly; no, I couldna tak' it in hand to sell six pennyworth of that ginger cake and let one and sixpence worth gae dry in the bakery— A beautiful day, mam! Won'erful blest in weather ye are! Let me open your umbrella for you, mam!"

. . . .

David Robb is the weaver of Pettybaw. All day long he sits at his old-fashioned hand-loom, which, like the fruit of his toil and the dear old graybeard himself, belongs to a day that is past and gone.

He might have work enough to keep an apprentice busy, but where would he find a lad sufficiently behind the times to learn a humble trade now banished to the limbo of superseded, almost forgotten things?

His home is but a poor place, but the rough room in which he works is big enough to hold a deal of sweet content. It is cheery enough, too, to attract the Pettybaw weans, who steal in on wet days and sit on the floor playing with the thrums, or with bits of colored ravelings. Sometimes when they have proved themselves wise and prudent little virgins, they are even allowed to touch the hanks of pink and yellow and blue yarn that lie in rainbow-hued confusion on the long deal table.

All this time the "heddles" go up and down, up and down, with their ceaseless clatter, and David throws the shuttle back and forth as he weaves his old-fashioned winseys.

We have grown to be good friends, David and I, and I have been permitted the signal honor of painting him at his work.

The loom stands by an eastern window, and the rare Pettybaw sunshine filters through the branches of a tree, shines upon the dusty window-panes, and throws a halo round David's head that he well deserves and little suspects. In my foreground sit Meg and Jean and Elspeth playing with thrums and wearing the fruit of David's loom in their gingham frocks. David himself sits on his wooden bench behind the maze of cords that form the "loom harness."

The snows of seventy winters powder his hair and beard. His spectacles are often pushed back on his kindly brow, but no glass could wholly obscure the clear integrity and steadfast purity of his eyes; and as for his smile I have not the art to paint that! It holds in solution so many sweet though humble virtues of patience, temperance, self-denial, honest endeavor, that my brush falters in the attempt to fix the radiant whole upon the canvas. Fashions come and go, modern improvements transform the arts and trades, manual skill gives way to the cunning of the machine, but old David Robb, after more than fifty years of toil, still sits at his hand-loom and weaves his winseys for the Pettybaw bairnies.

David has small book-learning, so he tells me; and indeed he had need to tell me, for I should never have discovered it myself, — one misses it so little when the larger things are all present!

A certain summer visitor in Pettybaw (a compatriot of ours, by the way) bought a quantity of David's orange-colored winsey, and finding that it wore like iron, wished to order more. She used the word "reproduce" in her telegram, as there was one pattern and one color she specially liked. Perhaps the context was not illuminating, but at any rate the word "reproduce" was not in David's vocabulary, and putting back his spectacles he told me his difficulty in deciphering the exact meaning of his fine-lady patron. He called at the Free kirk manse, — the meenister was no at hame; then to the library, — it was closed; then to the Established manse, —

the meenister was awa'. At last he obtained a glance at the schoolmaster's dictionary, and turning to "reproduce" found that it meant "*naught but mak' ower again;*" — and with an amused smile at the bedevilments of language he turned once more to his loom and I to my canvas.

Notwithstanding his unfamiliarity with langnebbit words, David has absorbed a deal of wisdom in his quiet life; though so far as I can see, his only books have been the green tree outside his window, a glimpse of the distant ocean, and the toil of his hands.

But I sometimes question if as many scholars are not made as marred in this wise, for, — to the seeing eye, — the waving leaf and the far sea, the daily task, one's own heart-beats, and one's neighbor's, — these teach us in good time to interpret Nature's secrets, and man's, and God's as well.

XX

> "The knights they harpit in their bow'r,
>   The ladyes sew'd and sang;
>   The mirth that was in that chamber
>   Through all the place it rang."
> *Rose the Red and White Lily.*

TEA at Rowardennan Castle is an impressive and a delightful function. It is served by a ministerial-looking butler and a just-ready-to-be-ordained footman. They both look as if they had been nourished on the Thirty-Nine Articles, but they know their business as well as if they had been trained in heathen lands,—which is saying a good deal, for everybody knows that heathen servants wait upon one with idolatrous solicitude. However, from the quality of the cheering beverage itself down to the thickness of the cream, the thinness of the china, the crispness of the toast, and the plummyness of the cake, tea at Rowardennan Castle is perfect in every detail.

The scones are of unusual lightness, also. I should think they would scarcely weigh more than four, perhaps even five, to a pound; but I am aware that the casual traveler, who eats only at hotels, and never has the privilege of entering feudal castles, will be slow to believe this estimate, particularly just after breakfast.

Salemina always describes a Scotch scone as an aspiring but unsuccessful soda biscuit of the New England sort. Stevenson, in writing of that dense black substance, inimical to life, called Scotch bun, says that the patriotism that leads a Scotsman to eat it will hardly desert him in any emergency. Salemina thinks that the scone should be bracketed with the bun (in description, of course, never in the human stomach), and says that, as a matter of fact, "th' unconquer'd Scot" of old was not only clad in a shirt of mail, but well fortified within when he went forth to warfare after a meal of oatmeal and scones. She insists that the spear which would pierce the shirt of mail would be turned aside and blunted by the ordinary scone of commerce; but what signifies the opinion of a woman who eats sugar on her porridge?

Considering the air of liberal hospitality that hangs about the castle tea-table, I wonder that our friends do not oftener avail themselves of its privileges and allow us to do so; but on all dark, foggy, or inclement days, or whenever they tire of the sands, everybody persists in taking tea at Bide-a-Wee Cottage.

We buy our tea of the Pettybaw grocer, some of our cups are cracked, the teapot is of earthenware, Miss Grieve disapproves of all social tea-fuddles and shows it plainly when she brings in the tray, and the room is so small that some of us overflow into the hall or the garden; it matters not; there is some fatal charm in our humble hospitality. At four o'clock one of us is obliged to be, like Sister Anne, on the housetop; and if company approaches, she must descend and speed to the plumber's for sixpenny worth extra of cream. In most well-ordered British households Miss Grieve would be requested to do this speeding, but both her mind and her body move too slowly for such domestic crises; and then, too, her temper has to be kept as unruffled as possible, so that she will cut the bread and butter thin. This she generally does if she has not been "fair doun-hadden wi' wark;" but the washing of her own spinster cup and plate, together with the incident sighs and groans, occupies her till so late an hour that she is not always dressed for callers.

Willie and I were reading "The Lady of the Lake," the other day, in the back garden, surrounded by the verdant leafage of our own kailyard. It is a pretty spot when the sun shines, a trifle domestic in its air, perhaps, but restful: Miss Grieve's dish-towels and aprons drying on the currant bushes, the cat playing with a mutton-bone or a fishtail on the grass, and the little birds perching on the rims of our wash-boiler and water-buckets. It can be reached only by way of the kitchen, which somewhat lessens its value as a pleasure-ground or a rustic retreat, but

Willie and I retire there now and then for a quiet chat.

On this particular occasion Willie was declaiming the exciting verses where FitzJames and Murdoch are crossing the stream

> "That joins Loch Katrine to Achray,"

where the crazed Blanche of Devan first appears: —

> "All in the Trosachs' glen was still,
> Noontide was sleeping on the hill:
> Sudden his guide whoop'd loud and high —
> 'Murdoch! was that a signal cry?'"

"It was indeed," said Francesca, appearing suddenly at an upper window overhanging the garden. "Pardon this intrusion, but the castle people are here," she continued in what is known as a stage whisper, — that is, one that can be easily heard by a thousand persons, — "the castle people and the ladies from Pettybaw House; and Mr. Macdonald is coming down the loaning; but Calamity Jane is making her toilette in the kitchen, and you cannot take Mr. Beresford through into the sitting-room at present. She says this hoose has so few conveniences that it's 'fair sickenin'.'"

"How long will she be?" queried Mr. Beresford anxiously, putting "The Lady of the Lake" in his pocket, and pacing up and down between the rows of cabbages.

"She has just begun. Whatever you do,

don't unsettle her temper, for she will have to prepare for eight to-day. I will send Mr. Macdonald and Miss Macrae to the bakery for gingerbread, to gain time, and possibly I can think of a way to rescue you. If I can't, are you tolerably comfortable? Perhaps Miss Grieve won't mind Penelope, and she can come through the kitchen any time and join us; but naturally you don't want to be separated, that's the worst of being engaged. Of course I can lower your tea in a tin bucket, and if it should rain I can throw out umbrellas. Would you like your golf-cape, Pen? 'Won'erful blest in weather ye are, mam!' The situation is not so bad as it might be," she added consolingly, " because in case Miss Grieve's toilette should last longer than usual, your wedding need not be indefinitely postponed, for Mr. Macdonald can marry you from this window."

Here she disappeared, and we had scarcely time to take in the full humor of the affair before Robin Anstruther's laughing eyes appeared over the top of the high brick wall that protects our garden on three sides.

"Do not shoot," said he. "I am not come to steal the fruit, but to succor humanity in distress. Miss Monroe insisted that I should borrow the inn ladder. She thought a rescue would be much more romantic than waiting for Miss Grieve. Everybody is coming out to witness it, at least all your guests,—there are no strangers present,—and Miss Monroe is already collecting sixpence a head for the entertainment, to be given, she says, to Mr. Macdonald's sustentation fund."

He was now astride of the wall, and speedily lifted the ladder to our side, where it leaned comfortably against the stout branches of the draper's peach vine. Willie ran nimbly up the ladder and bestrode the wall. I followed, first standing, and then decorously sitting down on the top of it. Mr. Anstruther pulled up the ladder, and replaced it on the side of liberty; then he descended, then Willie, and I last of all, amidst the acclamations of the on-lookers, a select company of six or eight persons.

When Miss Grieve formally entered the sitting-room bearing the tea-tray, she was buskit braw in black stuff gown, clean apron, and fresh cap trimmed with purple ribbons, under which her white locks were neatly dressed.

She deplored the coolness of the tea, but accounted for it to me in an aside by the sickening quality of Mrs. Sinkler's coals and Mr. Macbrose's kindling-wood, to say nothing of the insulting draft in the draper's range. When she left the room, I suppose she was unable to explain the peals of laughter that rang through our circumscribed halls.

Lady Ardmore insists that the rescue was the

most unique episode she ever witnessed, and says that she never understood America until she made our acquaintance. I persuaded her that this was fallacious reasoning; that while she might understand us by knowing America, she could not possibly reverse this mental operation and be sure of the result. The ladies of Pettybaw House said that the occurrence was as Fifish as anything that ever happened in Fife. The kingdom of Fife is noted, it seems, for its "doocots [dovecotes] and its daft lairds," and to be eccentric and Fifish are one and the same thing. Thereupon Francesca told Mr. Macdonald a story she heard in Edinburgh, to the effect that when a certain committee or council was quarreling as to which of certain Fifeshire towns should be the seat of a projected lunatic asylum, a new resident arose and suggested that the building of a wall round the kingdom of Fife would solve the difficulty, settle all disputes, and give sufficient room for the lunatics to exercise properly.

This is the sort of tale that a native can tell with a genial chuckle, but it comes with poor grace from an American lady sojourning in Fife. Francesca does not mind this, however, as she is at present avenging fresh insults to her own beloved country.

XXI

"With mimic din of stroke and ward
The broadsword upon target jarr'd."
The Lady of the Lake.

ROBIN ANSTRUTHER was telling stories at the tea-table.

"I got acquainted with an American girl in rather a queer sort of way," he said, between cups. "It was in London, on the Duke of York's wedding-day. I'm rather a tall chap, you see, and in the crowd somebody touched me on the shoulder and a plaintive voice behind me said, 'You're such a big man, and I am so little, will you please help me to save my life? My mother was separated from me in the crowd somewhere as we were trying to reach the Berkeley, and I don't know what to do.' I was a trifle nonplused, but I did the best I could. She was a tiny thing, in a marvelous frock and a flowery hat and a silver girdle and chatelaine. In another minute she spied a second man, an officer, a full head taller than I am, broad shoulders, splendidly put up altogether. Bless me! if she didn't turn to him and say, 'Oh, you're so nice and big, you're even bigger than this other gentleman, and I need you both in this dreadful crush. If you'll be good enough to stand on either side of me, I shall be awfully obliged.' We exchanged amused glances of embarrassment over her blonde head, but there was no resisting the irresistible. She was a small person, but she had the soul of a general, and we obeyed orders. We stood guard over her little ladyship for nearly an hour, and I must say she entertained us thoroughly, for she was as clever as she was pretty. Then I got her a seat in one of the windows of my club, while the other man, armed with a full description, went out to hunt up the mother; and by Jove! he found her, too. She would have her mother, and her mother she had. They were awfully jolly people; they came to luncheon in my chambers at the Albany afterwards, and we grew to be great friends."

"I dare say she was an English girl masquerading," I remarked facetiously. "What made you think her an American?"

"Oh, her general appearance and accent, I suppose."

"Probably she did n't say Barkley," observed Francesca cuttingly; "she would have been sure to commit that sort of solecism."

"Why, don't you say Barkley in the States?"

"Certainly not; we never call them the States, and with us c-l-e-r-k spells clerk, and B-e-r-k Berk."

"How very odd!" remarked Mr. Anstruther.

"No odder than your saying Bark, and not half as odd as your calling it Ălbany," I interpolated, to help Francesca.

"Quite so," said Mr. Anstruther; "but how do you say Ălbany in America?"

"Penelope and I allways call it Allbany," responded Francesca nonsensically, "but Salemina, who has been much in England, ălways calls it Ălbany."

This anecdote was the signal for Miss Ardmore to remark (apropos of her own discrimination and the American accent) that hearing a lady ask for a certain med'cine in a chemist's shop, she noted the intonation, and inquired of the chemist, when the fair stranger had retired, if she were not an American. "And she was!" exclaimed the Honorable Elizabeth triumphantly. "And what makes it the more curious, she had been over here twenty years, and of course spoke English quite properly."

In avenging fancied insults, it is certainly more just to heap punishment on the head of the real offender than upon his neighbor, and it is a trifle difficult to decide why Francesca should chastise Mr. Macdonald for the good-humored sins of Mr. Anstruther and Miss Ardmore; yet she does so, nevertheless.

The history of these chastisements she recounts in the nightly half-hour which she spends with me when I am endeavoring to compose myself for sleep. Francesca is fluent at all times, but once seated on the foot of my bed she becomes eloquent!

"It all began with his saying"—

This is her perennial introduction, and I respond as invariably, "What began?"

"Oh, to-day's argument with Mr. Macdonald. It was a literary quarrel this afternoon."

"'Fools rush in'"—I quoted.

"There is a good deal of nonsense in that old saw," she interrupted; "at all events, the most foolish fools I have ever known stayed still and did n't do anything. Rushing shows a certain movement of the mind, even if it is in the wrong direction. However, Mr. Macdonald is both opinionated and dogmatic, but his worst enemy could never call him a fool."

"I did n't allude to Mr. Macdonald."

"Don't you suppose I know to whom you alluded, dear? Is not your style so simple, frank, and direct that a wayfaring girl can read it and not err therein? No, I am not sitting on your feet, and it is not time to go to sleep; I wonder you do not tire of making these futile protests. As a matter of fact, we began this literary discussion yesterday morning, but were interrupted; and knowing that it was sure to come up again, I prepared for it with Salemina. She furnished the ammunition, so to speak, and I fired the guns."

"You always make so much noise with blank cartridges I wonder you ever bother about real shot," I remarked.

"Penelope, how can you abuse me when I am in trouble? Well, Mr. Macdonald was prating, as usual, about the antiquity of Scotland and its æons of stirring history. I am so weary of the venerableness of this country. How old will it have to be, I wonder, before it gets used to it? If it's the province of art to conceal art, it ought to be the province of age to conceal age, and it generally is. 'Everything does n't improve with years,' I observed sententiously.

"'For instance?' he inquired.

"Of course you know how that question affected me! How I do dislike an appetite for specific details! It is simply paralyzing to a good conversation. Do you remember that silly game in which some one points a stick at you and says, 'Beast, bird, or fish,—*beast!*' and you have to name one while he counts ten? If a beast has been requested, you can think of one fish and two birds, but no beasts. If he says '*Fish*,' all the beasts in the universe stalk through your memory, but not one finny, scaly, swimming thing! Well, that is the effect of 'For instance?' on my faculties. So I stumbled a bit, and succeeded in recalling, as objects which do not improve with age, mushrooms, women, and chickens, and he was obliged to agree with me, which nearly killed him. Then I said that although America is so fresh and blooming that people persist in calling it young, it is much older than it appears to the superficial eye. There is no real propriety in dating us as a nation from the Declaration of Independence in 1776, I said, nor even from the landing of the Pilgrims in 1620; nor, for that matter, from Columbus's discovery in 1492. It's my opinion, I asserted, that some of us had been there thousands of years before, but nobody had had the sense to discover us. We could n't discover ourselves, — though if we could have foreseen how the sere and yellow nations of the earth would taunt us with youth and inexperience, we should have had to do something desperate!"

"That theory must have been very convincing to the philosophic Scots mind," I interjected.

"It was; even Mr. Macdonald thought it ingenious. 'And so,' I went on, 'we were alive and awake and beginning to make history when you Scots were only barelegged savages roaming over the hills and stealing cattle. It was a very bad habit of yours, that cattle-stealing, and one which you kept up too long.'

"' No worse a sin than your stealing land from the Indians,' he said.

"' Oh yes,' I answered, 'because it was a smaller one! Yours was a vice, and ours a sin; or I mean it would have been a sin had we done it; but in reality we did n't steal land; we just *took* it, reserving plenty for the Indians to play about on; and for every hunting-ground we took away we gave them in exchange a serviceable plough, or a school, or a nice Indian agent, or something. That was land-grabbing, if you like, but it is a habit you Britishers have still, while we gave it up when we reached years of discretion.'"

"This is very illuminating," I interrupted, now thoroughly wide awake, "but it is n't my idea of a literary discussion."

"I am coming to that," she responded. "It was just at this point that, goaded into secret fury by my innocent speech about cattle-stealing, he began to belittle American literature, the poetry especially. Of course he waxed eloquent about the royal line of poet-kings that had made his country famous, and said the people who could claim Shakespeare had reason to be the proudest nation on earth. 'Doubtless,' I said. 'But do you mean to say that Scotland has any nearer claim upon Shakespeare than we have? I do not now allude to the fact that in the large sense he is the common property of the English-speaking world' (Salemina told me to say that), 'but Shakespeare died in 1616, and the union of Scotland with England did n't come about till 1707, nearly a century afterwards. You really have n't anything to do with him! But as for us, we did n't leave England until 1620, when Shakespeare had been perfectly dead four years. We took very good care not to come away too soon. Chaucer and Spenser were dead, too, and we had nothing to stay for!'"

I was obliged to relax here and give vent to a burst of merriment at Francesca's absurdities.

"I could see that he had never regarded the matter in that light before," she went on gayly, encouraged by my laughter, "but he braced himself for the conflict, and said, 'I wonder that you did n't stay a little longer while you were about it. Milton and Ben Jonson were still alive; Bacon's Novum Organum was just coming out; and in thirty or forty years you could have had L'Allegro, Il Penseroso, and Paradise Lost; Newton's Principia, too, in 1687. Perhaps these were all too serious and heavy for your national taste; still, one sometimes likes to claim things one cannot fully appreciate. And then, too, if you had once begun to stay, waiting for the great things to happen and the great books to be written, you would never have gone, for there would still have been Browning, Tennyson, and Swinburne to delay you.'

"'If we could n't stay to see out your great bards, we certainly could n't afford to remain and welcome your minor ones,' I answered frigidly; 'but we wanted to be well out of the way before England united with Scotland, knowing that if we were uncomfortable as things were, it would be a good deal worse after the Union; and we had to come home, anyway, and start our own poets. Emerson, Whittier, Longfellow, Holmes, and Lowell had to be born.'

"'I suppose they had to be if you had set your mind on it,' he said, 'though personally I could have spared one or two on that roll of honor.'

"'Very probably,' I remarked, as thoroughly angry now as he intended I should be. 'We cannot expect you to appreciate all the American poets; indeed, you cannot appreciate all of your own, for the same nation does n't always furnish the writers and the readers. Take your precious Browning, for example! There are hundreds of Browning Clubs in America, and I never heard of a single one in Scotland.'

"'No,' he retorted, 'I dare say; but there is a good deal in belonging to a people who can understand him without clubs!'"

"Oh, Francesca!" I exclaimed, sitting bolt upright among my pillows. "How could you give him that chance! How *could* you! What did you say?"

"I said nothing," she replied mysteriously. "I did something much more to the point, — I cried!"

"*Cried?*"

"Yes, cried; not rivers and freshets of woe, but small brooks and streamlets of helpless mortification."

"What did he do then?"

"Why do you say 'do'?"

"Oh, I mean 'say,' of course. Don't trifle; go on. What did he say then?"

"There are some things too dreadful to describe," she answered, and wrapping her Italian blanket majestically about her she retired to her own apartment, shooting one enigmatical glance at me as she closed the door.

That glance puzzled me for some time after she left the room. It was as expressive and interesting a beam as ever darted from a woman's eye. The combination of elements involved in it, if an abstract thing may be conceived as existing in component parts, was something like this:—

One half, mystery.

One eighth, triumph.

One eighth, amusement.

One sixteenth, pride.

One sixteenth, shame.

One sixteenth, desire to confess.

One sixteenth, determination to conceal.

And all these delicate, complex emotions played together in a circle of arching eyebrow, curving lip, and tremulous chin,— played together, mingling and melting into one another like fire and snow; bewildering, mystifying, enchanting the beholder!

If Ronald Macdonald did — I am a woman, but, for one, I can hardly blame him!

XXII

> "'O has he chosen a bonny bride,
>   An' has he clean forgotten me?'
>   An' sighing said that gay ladye,
>   'I would I were in my ain countrie!'"
>   *Lord Beichan.*

It rained in torrents; Salemina was darning stockings in the inglenook at Bide-a-Wee Cottage, and I was reading her a Scotch letter which Francesca and I had concocted the evening before. I proposed sending the document to certain chosen spirits in our own country, who were pleased to be facetious concerning our devotion to Scotland. It contained, in sooth, little that was new, and still less that was true, for we were confined to a very small vocabulary which we were obliged to supplement now and then by a dip into Burns and Allan Ramsay.

Here is the letter:—

Bide-a-Wee Cottage,
Pettybaw.
East Neuk o' Fife.

To my trusty Fieres,— Mony's the time I hae ettled to send ye a screed, but there was aye something that cam' i' the gait. It wisna that I couldna be fashed, for aften hae I thocht o' ye and my hairt has been wi' ye mony 's the day. There 's no muckle fowk frae Ameriky hereawa; they 're a' jist Fife bodies, and a lass canna get her tongue roun' their thrapple-taxin' words ava, so it 's like I may een drap a' the sweetness o' my good mither-tongue.

'T is a dulefu' nicht, and an awful blash is ragin' wi'oot. Fanny 's awa' at the gowff rinnin' aboot wi' a bag o' sticks after a wee bit ba', and Sally and I are hame by oor lane. Laith will the lassie be to weet her bonny shoon, but lang ere the play 'll be o'er, she 'll wat her hat aboon. A gust o' win' is skirlin' the noo, and as we luik ower the faem, the haar is risin', weetin' the green swaird wi' misty shoo'rs.

Yestreen was a calm simmer gloamin', sae sweet an' bonnie that while the sun was sinkin' doon ower Pettybaw Sands, we daundered ower the muir. As we cam' through the scented birks, we saw a trottin' burnie wimplin' 'neath the white-blossomed slaes and hirplin' doon the hillside; an' while a herd-laddie lilted ower the fernie brae, a cushat crooed leesomely doon i' the dale. We pit aff oor shoon, sae blithe were we, kilted oor coats a little aboon the knee and paidilt i' the burn, gettin' gey an' weet the while. Then Sally pu'd the gowans wat wi' dew an' twined her bree wi' tasseled broom, while I had a wee crackie wi' Tibby Buchan, the flesher's dochter frae Auld Reekie. Tibby 's nae giglet gawky like the lave, ye ken, — she's a sonsie maid, as sweet as ony hinny pear, wi' her twa pawky een an' her cockernony snooded up fu' sleek.

We were unco gleg to win hame when a' this was dune, an' after steekin' the door, to sit an' taist oor taes at the bit blaze. Mickle thocht we o' the gentles ayont the sea an' sair grat we for a' frien's we knew lang syne in oor ain countree.

Late at nicht, Fanny, the bonny gypsy, cam' ben the hoose an' tirled at the pin of oor bigly bower door, speirin' for baps and bannocks.

"Hoots, lassie!" cried oot Sally, "th' auld carline i' the kitchen is i' her box-bed an' weel aneuch ye ken is lang syne cuddled doon."

"Oo, ay!" said Fanny, straikin' her curly pow, "then fetch me parritch an' dinna be lang wi' 'em, for I've lickit a Pettybaw lass at the gowff, an' I could eat twa guid jints o' beef gin I had 'em!"

"Losh, girl," said I, "gie ower makin' sic a mickle din. Ye ken verra weel ye'll get nae parritch the nicht. I'll rin an' fetch ye a 'piece' to stap awee the soun'."

"Blathers an' havers!" cried Fanny, but she blinkit bonnily the while, an' when the tea was weel maskit, she smoored her wrath an' stappit her mooth wi' a bit o' oaten cake. We aye keep that i' the hoose, for th' auld servant-body is gey an' bad at the cookin' an' she's sae dour an' dowie that to speak but till her we daur hardly mint.

In sic divairsions pass the lang simmer days in braid Scotland, but I canna write mair the nicht, for 't is the wee sma' hours ayont the twal'.

Like th' auld wife's parrot, "we dinna speak muckle, but we 're deevils to think," an' we 're aye thinkin' aboot ye. An' noo I maun leave ye to mak' what ye can oot o' this, for I jalouse it 'll pass ye to untaukle the whole hypothec.

Fair fa' ye a'! Lang may yer lum reek, an' may prosperity attend oor clan!

Aye your gude frien',
PENELOPE HAMILTON.

"It may be very fine," remarked Salemina judicially, "though I cannot understand more than half of it."

"That would also be true of Browning," I replied. "Don't you love to see great ideas loom through a mist of words?"

"The words are misty enough in this case," she said, "and I do wish you would not tell the world that I paddle in the burn, or 'twine my bree wi' tasseled broom.' I 'm too old to be made ridiculous."

"Nobody will believe it," said Francesca appearing in the doorway. "They will know it is only Penelope's havering," and with this undeserved scoff, she took her mashie and went golfing; not on the links, on this occasion, but in our microscopic sitting-room. It is twelve feet square, and holds a tiny piano, desk, centre-table, sofa, and chairs, but the spot between the fireplace and the table is Francesca's favorite "putting green." She wishes to become more deadly in the matter of approaches, and thinks her tee shots weak; so these two deficiencies she is trying to make good by home practice in inclement weather. She turns a tumbler on its side on the floor, and "puts" the ball into it, or at it, as the case may be, from the opposite side of the room. It is excellent discipline, and as the tumblers are inexpensive the breakage really does not matter. Whenever Miss Grieve hears the shivering of glass, she murmurs, not without reason, "It is not for the knowing what they will be doing next."

"Penelope, has it ever occurred to you that Elizabeth Ardmore is seriously interested in Mr. Macdonald?"

Salemina propounded this question to me with the same innocence that a babe would display in placing a match beside a dynamite bomb.

Francesca naturally heard the remark, — although it was addressed to me, — pricked up her ears, and missed the tumbler by several feet.

It was a simple inquiry, but as I look back upon it from the safe ground of subsequent knowledge I perceive that it had a certain amount of influence upon Francesca's history. The suggestion would have carried no weight with me for two reasons. In the first place, Salemina is farsighted. If objects are located at some distance from her, she sees them clearly; but if they are under her very nose she overlooks them altogether, unless they are sufficiently fragrant or audible to address other senses. This physical peculiarity she carries over into her mental processes. Her impression of the Disruption movement, for example, would be lively and distinct, but her perception of a contemporary lovers' quarrel (particularly if it were fought at her own apron-strings) would be singularly vague. If she suggested, therefore, that Elizabeth Ardmore was interested in Mr. Beresford, who is the rightful captive of my bow and spear, I should be perfectly calm.

My second reason for comfortable indifference is that, frequently in novels, and always in plays, the heroine is instigated to violent jealousy by insinuations of this sort, usually conveyed by the villain of the piece, male or female. I have seen this happen so often in the modern drama that it has long since ceased to be convincing; but though Francesca has witnessed scores of plays and read hundreds of novels, it did not apparently strike her as a theatrical or literary suggestion that Lady Ardmore's daughter should be in love with Mr. Macdonald. The effect of the new point of view was most salutary, on the whole. She had come to think herself the only prominent figure in the Reverend Ronald's landscape, and anything more impertinent than her tone with him (unless it is his with her) I certainly never heard. This criticism, however, relates only to their public performances, and I have long suspected that their private conversations are of a kindlier character. When it occurred to her that he might simply be sharpening his mental sword on her steel, but that his heart had at last wandered into a more genial climate than she had ever provided for it, she softened unconsciously; the Scotsman and the American receded into a truer perspective, and the man and the woman approached each other with dangerous nearness.

"What shall we do if Francesca and Mr. Macdonald really fall in love with each other?" asked Salemina, when Francesca had gone into the hall to try long drives. (There is a good deal of excitement in this, as Miss Grieve has to cross the passage on her way from the kitchen to the china-closet, and thus often serves as a reluctant "hazard" or "bunker.")

"Do you mean what should we have done?" I queried.

"Nonsense, don't be captious! It can't be too late yet. They have known each other only a little over two months; when would you have had me interfere, pray?"

"It depends upon what you expect to accomplish. If you wish to stop the marriage, interfere in a fortnight or so; if you wish to prevent an engagement, speak — well, say to-morrow; if, however, you did n't wish them to fall in love with each other, you should have kept one of them away from Lady Baird's dinner."

"I could have waited a trifle longer than that," argued Salemina, "for you remember how badly they got on at first."

"I remember you thought so," I responded dryly; "but I believe Mr. Macdonald has been interested in Francesca from the outset, partly because her beauty and vivacity attracted him, partly because he could keep her in order only by putting his whole mind upon her. On his side, he has succeeded in piquing her into thinking of him continually, though solely, as she fancies, for the purpose of crossing swords with him. If they ever drop their weapons for an instant, and allow the din of warfare to subside so that they can listen to their own heart-beats, they will discover that they love each other to distraction."

"Ye ken mair than 's in the catecheesm," remarked Salemina, yawning a little as she put away her darning-ball. "It is pathetic to see you waste your time painting mediocre pictures, when as a lecturer upon love you could instruct your thousands."

"The thousands would never satisfy me," I retorted, "so long as you remained uninstructed, for in your single person you would so swell the sum of human ignorance on that subject that my teaching would be forever vain."

"Very clever indeed! Well, what will Mr. Monroe say to me when I land in New York without his daughter, or with his son-in-law?"

"He has never denied Francesca anything in her life; why should he draw the line at a Scotsman? I am much more concerned about Mr. Macdonald's congregation."

"I am not anxious about that," said Salemina loyally. "Francesca would be the life of an Inchcaldy parish."

"I dare say," I observed, "but she might be the death of the pastor."

"I am ashamed of you, Penelope; or I should be if you meant what you say. She can make the people love her if she tries; when did she ever fail at that? But with Mr. Macdonald's talent, to say nothing of his family connections, he is sure to get a church in Edinburgh in a few years, if he wishes. Undoubtedly, it would not be a great match in a money sense. I suppose he has a manse and three or four hundred pounds a year."

"That sum would do nicely for cabs."

"Penelope, you are flippant!"

"I don't mean it, dear; it's only for fun; and

it would be so absurd if we should leave Francesca over here as the presiding genius of an Inchcaldy parsonage, — I mean a manse!"

"It is n't as if she were penniless," continued Salemina; "she has fortune enough to assure her own independence, and not enough to threaten his, — the ideal amount. I hardly think the good Lord's first intention was to make her a minister's wife, but he knows very well that Love is a master architect. Francesca is full of beautiful possibilities if Mr. Macdonald is the man to bring them out, and I am inclined to think he is."

"He has brought out impishness so far," I objected.

"The impishness is transitory," she returned, "and I am speaking of permanent qualities. His is the stronger and more serious nature, Francesca's the sweeter and more flexible. He will be the oak-tree, and she will be the sunshine playing in the branches."

"Salemina, dear," I said penitently, kissing her gray hair, "I apologize: you are not absolutely ignorant about Love, after all, when you call him the master architect; and that is very lovely and very true about the oak-tree and the sunshine."

XXIII

"' Love, I maun gang to Edinbrugh,
  Love, I maun gang an' leave thee!'
  She sighed right sair, an' said nae mair
  But ' O gin I were wi' ye!'"
                                Andrew Lammie.

JEAN DALZIEL came to visit us a week ago, and has put new life into our little circle. I suppose it was playing " Sir Patrick Spens " that set us thinking about it, for one warm, idle day when we were all in the Glen we began a series of ballad-revels, in which each of us assumed a favorite character. The choice induced so much argument and disagreement that Mr. Beresford was at last appointed head of the clan; and having announced himself formally as the Mackintosh, he was placed on the summit of a hastily arranged pyramidal cairn. He was given an ash wand and a rowan-tree sword; and then, according to ancient custom, his pedigree and the exploits of his ancestors were recounted, and he was exhorted to emulate their example. Now it seems that a Highland chief of the olden time, being as absolute in his patriarchal authority as any prince, had a corresponding number of officers attached to his person. He had a bodyguard, who fought around him in battle, and independent of this he had a staff of officers who accompanied him wherever he went. These our chief proceeded to appoint as follows: —

Henchman, Ronald Macdonald; bard, Penelope Hamilton; spokesman or fool, Robin Anstruther; sword-bearer, Francesca Monroe; piper, Salemina; piper's attendant, Elizabeth Ardmore; baggage gillie, Jean Dalziel; running footman, Ralph; bridle gillie, Jamie; ford gillie, Miss Grieve. The ford gillie carries the chief across fords only, and there are no fords in the vicinity; so Mr. Beresford, not liking to leave a member of our household out of office, thought this the best post for Calamity Jane.

With the Mackintosh on his pyramidal cairn matters went very much better, and at Jamie's instigation we began to hold rehearsals for certain festivities at Rowardennan; for as Jamie's birthday fell on the eve of the Queen's Jubilee, there was to be a gay party at the castle.

All this occurred days ago, and yesterday evening the ballad-revels came off, and Rowardennan was a scene of great pageant and splendor. Lady Ardmore, dressed as the Lady of Inverleith, received the guests, and there were all manner of tableaux, and ballads in costume, and pantomimes, and a grand march by the clan, in which we appeared in our chosen rôles.

Salemina was Lady Maisry, — she whom all the lords of the north countrie came wooing.

> "But a' that they could say to her,
> Her answer still was ' Na.' "

And again : —

> "' O haud your tongues, young men,' she said,
> ' And think nae mair on me ! ' "

Mr. Beresford was Lord Beichan, and I was Shusy Pye.

> " Lord Beichan was a Christian born,
> And such resolved to live and dee,
> So he was ta'en by a savage Moor,
> Who treated him right cruellie.

> " The Moor he had an only daughter,
> The damsel's name was Shusy Pye ;
> And ilka day as she took the air
> Lord Beichan's prison she pass'd by."

Elizabeth Ardmore was Leezie Lindsay, who kilted her coats o' green satin to the knee and was aff to the Hielands so expeditiously when her lover declared himself to be " Lord Ronald Macdonald, a chieftain of high degree."

Francesca was Mary Ambree.

> " When captaines couragious, whom death cold not daunte,
> Did march to the siege of the citty of Gaunt,
> They mustred their souldiers by two and by three,
> And the foremost in battle was Mary Ambree.

> " When the brave sergeant-major was slaine in her sight
> Who was her true lover, her joy and delight,
> Because he was slaine most treacherouslie,
> Then vow'd to avenge him Mary Ambree."

Brenda Macrae from Pettybaw House was

Fairly Fair; Jamie, Sir Patrick Spens; Ralph, King Alexander of Dunfermline; Mr. Anstruther, Bonnie Glenlogie, "the flower of them a';" Mr. Macdonald and Miss Dalziel, Young Hynde Horn and the king's daughter Jean respectively.

> "'Oh, it's Hynde Horn fair, and it's Hynde Horn free;
> Oh, where were you born, and in what countrie?'
> 'In a far distant countrie I was born;
> But of home and friends I am quite forlorn.'
>
> "Oh, it's seven long years he served the king,
> But wages from him he ne'er got a thing;
> Oh, it's seven long years he served, I ween,
> And all for love of the king's daughter Jean."

It is not to be supposed that all this went off without any of the difficulties and heart-burnings that are incident to things dramatic. When Elizabeth Ardmore chose to be Leezie Lindsay, she asked me to sing the ballad behind the scenes. Mr. Beresford naturally thought that Mr. Macdonald would take the opposite part in the tableau, inasmuch as the hero bears his name; but he positively declined to play Lord Ronald Macdonald, and said it was altogether too personal.

Mr. Anstruther was rather disagreeable at the beginning, and upbraided Miss Dalziel for offering to be the king's daughter Jean to Mr. Macdonald's Hynde Horn, when she knew very well he wanted her for Ladye Jeanie in Glenlogie. (She had meantime confided to me that nothing could induce her to appear in Glenlogie; it was far too personal.)

Mr. Macdonald offended Francesca by sending her his cast-off gown and begging her to be Sir Patrick Spens; and she was still more gloomy (so I imagined) because he had not proffered his six feet of manly beauty for the part of the captain in Mary Ambree, when the only other person to take it was Jamie's tutor. He is an Oxford man and a delightful person, but very bow-legged; added to that, by the time the rehearsals had ended she had been obliged to beg him to love some one more worthy than herself, and did not wish to appear in the same tableau with him, feeling that it was much too personal.

When the eventful hour came, yesterday, Willie and I were the only actors really willing to take lovers' parts, save Jamie and Ralph, who were but too anxious to play all the characters, whatever their age, sex, color, or relations. But the guests knew nothing of these trivial disagreements, and at ten o'clock last night it would have been difficult to match Rowardennan Castle for a scene of beauty and revelry. Everything went merrily till we came to Hynde Horn, the concluding tableau, and the most effective and elaborate one on the programme. At the very last moment, when the opening scene was nearly ready, Jean Dalziel fell down a secret staircase that led from the tapestry chamber into Lady Ardmore's boudoir, where the rest of us were dressing. It was a short flight of steps, but, as she held a candle and was carrying her costume, she fell awkwardly, spraining her wrist and ankle. Finding that she was not maimed for life, Lady Ardmore turned with comical and unsympathetic haste to Francesca, so completely do amateur theatricals dry the milk of kindness in the human breast.

"Put on these clothes at once," she said imperiously, knowing nothing of the volcanoes beneath the surface. "Hynde Horn is already on the stage, and somebody must be Jean. Take care of Miss Dalziel, girls, and ring for more maids. Hélène, help me dress Miss Monroe: put on her slippers while I lace her gown; run and fetch more jewels, — more still, — she can carry off any number; not any rouge, Hélène, — she has too much color now; pull the frock more off the shoulders, — it's a pity to cover an inch of them; pile her hair higher, — here, take my diamond tiara, child; hurry, Hélène, fetch the silver cup and the cake — no, they are on the stage; take her train, Hélène. Miss Hamilton, run and open the doors ahead of them, please. I won't go down for this tableau. I'll put Miss Dalziel right, and then I'll slip into the drawing-room, to be ready for the guests when they come in."

We hurried breathlessly through an interminable series of rooms and corridors. I gave the signal to Mr. Beresford, who was nervously waiting for it in the wings, and the curtain went up on Hynde Horn disguised as the auld beggar man at the king's gate. Mr. Beresford was reading the ballad, and we took up the tableaux at the point where Hynde Horn has come from a far countrie to see why the diamonds in the ring given him by his own true love have grown pale and wan. He hears that the king's daughter Jean has been married to a knight these nine days past.

> " But unto him a wife the bride winna be,
> For love of Hynde Horn, far over the sea."

He therefore borrows the old beggar's garments and hobbles to the king's palace, where he petitions the porter for a cup of wine and a bit of cake to be handed him by the fair bride herself.

> " ' Good porter, I pray, for Saints Peter and Paul,
> And for sake of the Saviour who died for us all,
> For one cup of wine, and one bit of bread,
> To an auld man with travel and hunger bestead.

> " ' And ask the fair bride, for the sake of Hynde Horn,
> To hand them to me so sadly forlorn.'
> Then the porter for pity the message convey'd,
> And told the fair bride all the beggar man said."

The curtain went up again. The porter, moved to pity, has gone to give the message to his lady. Hynde Horn is watching the staircase at the rear of the stage, his heart in his eyes. The tapestries that hide it are drawn, and there stands the king's daughter, who tripped down the stair,

> "And in her fair hands did lovingly bear
> A cup of red wine, and a farle of cake,
> To give the old man for loved Hynde Horn's sake."

The hero of the ballad, who had not seen his true love for seven long years, could not have been more amazed at the change in her than was Ronald Macdonald at the sight of the flushed, excited, almost tearful king's daughter on the staircase; Lady Ardmore's diamonds flashing from her crimson satin gown, Lady Ardmore's rubies glowing on her white arms and throat; not Miss Dalziel, as had been arranged, but Francesca, rebellious, reluctant, embarrassed, angrily beautiful and beautifully angry!

In the next scene Hynde Horn has drained the cup and dropped the ring into it.

> "'Oh, found you that ring by sea or on land,
> Or got you that ring off a dead man's hand?'
> 'Oh, I found not that ring by sea or on land,
> But I got that ring from a fair lady's hand.
>
> "'As a pledge of true love she gave it to me,
> Full seven years ago as I sail'd o'er the sea;
> But now that the diamonds are chang'd in their hue,
> I know that my love has to me proved untrue.'"

I never saw a prettier picture of sweet, tremulous womanhood, a more enchanting breathing image of fidelity, than Francesca looked as Mr. Beresford read:—

> "'Oh, I will cast off my gay costly gown,
> And follow thee on from town unto town,
> And I will take the gold kaims from my hair
> And follow my true love for ever mair.'"

Whereupon Hynde Horn lets his beggar weeds fall, and shines there the foremost and noblest of all the king's companie as he says:—

> "'You need not cast off your gay costly gown,
> To follow me on from town unto town;
> You need not take the gold kaims from your hair,
> For Hynde Horn has gold enough and to spare.'
>
> "Then the bridegrooms were chang'd, and the lady re-wed
> To Hynde Horn thus come back, like one from the dead."

There is no doubt that this tableau gained the success of the evening, and the participants in it should have modestly and gratefully received the choruses of congratulation that were ready to be offered during the supper and dance that followed. Instead of that, what happened? Francesca drove home with Miss Dalziel before the quadrille d'honneur, and when Willie bade me good-night at the gate in the loaning he said, "I shall not be early to-morrow, dear. I am going to see Macdonald off."

"Off!" I exclaimed. "Where is he going?"

"Only to Edinburgh and London, to stay till the last of next week."

"But we may have left Pettybaw by that time."

"Of course; that is probably what he has in mind. But let me tell you this, Penelope: Macdonald is fathoms deep in love with Francesca, and if she trifles with him she shall know what I think of her!"

"And let me tell you this, sir: Francesca is fathoms deep in love with Ronald Macdonald, little as you suspect it, and if he trifles with her he shall know what I think of him!"

XXIV

> "He set her on a coal-black steed,
>   Himsel lap on behind her,
> An' he's awa' to the Hieland hills
>   Whare her frien's they canna find her."
>
> *Rob Roy.*

THE occupants of Bide-a-Wee Cottage awoke in anything but a Jubilee humor, next day. Willie had intended to come at nine, but of course did not appear. Francesca took her breakfast in bed, and came listlessly into the sitting-room at ten o'clock, looking like a ghost. Jean's ankle was much better, — the sprain proved to be not even a strain, — but her wrist was painful. It was drizzling, too, and we had promised Miss Ardmore and Miss Macrae to aid with the last Jubilee decorations, the distribution of medals at the church, and the children's games and tea on the links in the afternoon.

We had determined not to desert our beloved Pettybaw for the metropolis on this great day, but to celebrate it with the dear fowk o' Fife who had grown to be a part of our lives.

Bide-a-Wee Cottage does not occupy an imposing position in the landscape, and the choice of art fabrics at the Pettybaw draper's is small, but the moment it should stop raining we were intending to carry out a dazzling scheme of decoration that would proclaim our affectionate respect for the "little lady in black" on her Diamond Jubilee. But would it stop raining? — that was the question. The draper wasna certain that so licht a shoo'r could richtly be called rain. The village weans were yearning for the hour to arrive when they might sit on the wet golf-course and have tea; manifestly, therefore, it could not be a bad day for Scotland; but if it should grow worse, what would become of our mammoth subscription bonfire on Pettybaw Law, — the bonfire that Brenda Macrae was to light, as the lady of the manor?

There were no deputations to request the honor of Miss Macrae's distinguished services on this occasion; that is not the way the self-respecting villager comports himself in Fifeshire. The chairman of the local committee, a respectable gardener, called upon Miss Macrae at Pettybaw House, and said, "I'm sent to tell ye ye're to have the pleesure an' the honor of lightin' the bonfire the nicht! Ay, it's a grand chance ye're havin', miss; ye'll remember it as long as ye live, I'm thinkin'!"

When I complimented this rugged soul on his decoration of the triumphal arch under which the schoolchildren were to pass, I said, "I think if her Majesty could see it, she would be pleased with our village to-day, James."

"Ay, ye 're richt, miss," he replied complacently. "She 'd see that Inchcawdy canna compeer wi' us; we 've patronized her weel in Pettybaw!"

Truly, as Stevenson says, "he who goes fishing among the Scots peasantry with condescension for a bait will have an empty basket by evening."

At eleven o'clock a boy arrived at Bide-a-Wee with an interesting-looking package, which I promptly opened. That dear foolish lover of mine (whose foolishness is one of the most adorable things about him) makes me only two visits a day, and is therefore constrained to send me some reminder of himself in the intervening hours, or minutes, — a book, a flower, or a note. Uncovering the pretty box, I found a long, slender — something — of sparkling silver.

"What is it?" I exclaimed, holding it up. "It is too long and not wide enough for a paper-knife, although it would be famous for cutting magazines. Is it a *bâton?* Where did Willie find it, and what can it be? There is something engraved on one side, something that looks like birds on a twig, — yes, three little birds; and see the lovely cairngorm set in the end! Oh, it has words cut in it: '*To Jean: From Hynde Horn*' — Goodness me! I 've opened Miss Dalziel's package!"

Francesca made a sudden swooping motion, and caught box, cover, and contents in her arms.

"It is mine! I know it is mine!" she cried. "You really ought not to claim everything that is sent to the house, Penelope, — as if nobody had any friends or presents but you!" and she rushed upstairs like a whirlwind.

I examined the outside wrapper, lying on the floor, and found, to my chagrin, that it did bear Miss Monroe's name, somewhat blotted by the rain; but if the box were addressed to her, why was the silver thing inscribed to Miss Dalziel? Well, Francesca would explain the mystery within the hour, unless she had become a changed being.

Fifteen minutes passed. Salemina was making Jubilee sandwiches at Pettybaw House, Miss Dalziel was asleep in her room, I was being devoured slowly by curiosity, when Francesca came down without a word, walked out of the front door, went up to the main street, and entered the village post-office without so much as a backward glance. She was a changed being, then! I might as well be living in a Gaboriau novel, I thought, and went up into my little painting and writing room to address a programme of the Pettybaw celebration to Lady Baird, watch for the first glimpse of Willie coming down the loaning, and see if I could discover where Francesca went from the post-office.

Sitting down by my desk, I could find neither my wax nor my silver candlestick, my scissors nor my ball of twine. Plainly, Francesca had been on one of her borrowing tours; and she had left an additional trace of herself — if one were needed — in a book of old Scottish ballads, open at Hynde Horn. I glanced at it idly while I was waiting for her to return. I was not familiar with the opening verses, and these were the first lines that met my eye : —

> "Oh, he gave to his love a silver wand,
> Her sceptre of rule over fair Scotland;
> With three singing laverocks set thereon
> For to mind her of him when he was gone.
>
> " And his love gave to him a gay gold ring
> With three shining diamonds set therein;
> Oh, his love gave to him this gay gold ring,
> Of virtue and value above all thing."

A light dawned upon me! The silver mystery, then, was intended for a wand, — and a very pretty way of making love to an American girl, too, to call it a "sceptre of rule over fair Scotland;" and the three birds were three singing laverocks "to mind her of him when he was gone!"

But the real Hynde Horn in the dear old ballad had a true love who was not captious and capricious and cold like Francesca. His love gave him a gay gold ring, —

> "Of virtue and value above all thing."

Yet stay: behind the ballad book flung heedlessly on my desk was — what should it be but the little morocco case, empty now, in which our Francesca keeps her dead mother's engagement ring, — the mother who died when she was a wee child. Truly a very pretty modern ballad to be sung in these unromantic, degenerate days!

Francesca came in at the door behind me, saw her secret reflected in my telltale face, saw the sympathetic moisture in my eyes, and, flinging herself into my willing arms, burst into tears.

"Oh, Pen, dear, dear Pen, I am so miserable and so happy; so afraid that he won't come back, so frightened for fear that he will! I sent him away because there were so many lions in the path, and I did n't know how to slay them. I thought of my f-father; I thought of my c-c-country. I did n't want to live with him in Scotland, I knew that I could n't live without him in America, and there I was! I did n't think I was s-suited to a minister, and I am not; but oh! this p-particular minister is so s-suited to me!" and she threw herself on the sofa and buried her head in the cushions.

She was so absurd even in her grief that I had hard work to keep from smiling.

"Let us talk about the lions," I said soothingly. "But when did the trouble begin? When did he speak to you?"

"After the tableaux last night; but of course there had been other — other — times — and things."

"Of course. Well?"

"He had told me a week before that he should go away for a while, that it made him too wretched to stay here just now; and I suppose that was when he got the silver wand ready for me. It was meant for the Jean of the poem, you know. Of course he would not put my own name on a gift like that."

"You don't think he had it made for Jean Dalziel in the first place?" I asked this, thinking she needed some sort of tonic in her relaxed condition.

"You know him better than that, Penelope! I am ashamed of you! We had read Hynde Horn together ages before Jean Dalziel came; but I imagine, when we came to acting the lines, he thought it would be better to have some other king's daughter; that is, that it would be less personal. And I never, never would have been in the tableau, if I had dared refuse Lady Ardmore, or could have explained; but I had no time to think. And then, naturally, he thought by my being there as the king's daughter that — that — the lions were slain, you know; instead of which they were roaring so that I could hardly hear the orchestra."

"Francesca, look me in the eye! Do — you — love him?"

"Love him? I adore him!" she exclaimed in good clear decisive English, as she rose impetuously and paced up and down in front of the sofa. "But in the first place there is the difference in nationality."

"I have no patience with you. One would think he was a Turk, an Esquimau, or a cannibal. He is white, he speaks English, and he believes in the Christian religion. The idea of calling such a man a foreigner!"

"Oh, it did n't prevent me from loving him," she confessed, "but I thought at first it would be unpatriotic to marry him."

"Did you think Columbia could not spare you even as a rare specimen to be used for exhibition purposes?" I asked wickedly.

"You know I am not so conceited as that! No," she continued ingenuously, "I feared that if I accepted him it would look, over here, as if the home supply of husbands were of inferior quality; and then we had such disagreeable discussions at the beginning, I simply could not bear to leave my nice new free country, and ally myself with his æons of tiresome history. But it came to me in the night, a week ago, that after all I should hate a man who did n't love his fatherland; and in the illumination of that new idea Ronald's character assumed a different outline in my mind. How could he love America when he had never seen it? How could I convince him that American women are the most charming in the world in any better way than by letting him live under the same roof with a good example? How could I expect him to let me love my country best unless I permitted him to love his best?"

"You need n't offer so many apologies for your infatuation, my dear," I answered dryly.

"I am not apologizing for it!" she exclaimed impulsively. "Oh, if you could only keep it to yourself, I should like to tell you how I trust and admire and reverence Ronald Macdonald, but of course you will repeat everything to Willie Beresford within the hour! You think he has gone on and on loving me against his better judgment. You believe he has fought against it because of my unfitness, but that I, poor, weak, trivial thing, am not capable of deep feeling and that I shall never appreciate the sacrifices he makes in choosing me! Very well, then, I tell you plainly that if I had to live in a damp manse the rest of my life, drink tea and eat scones for breakfast, and — and buy my hats of the Inchcaldy milliner, I should still glory in the possibility of being Ronald Macdonald's wife, — a possibility hourly growing more uncertain, I am sorry to say!"

"And the extreme aversion with which you began," I asked, — "what has become of that, and when did it begin to turn in the opposite direction?"

"Aversion!" she cried, with convincing and unblushing candor. "That aversion was a cover, clapped on to keep my self-respect warm. I abused him a good deal, it is true, because it was so delightful to hear you and Salemina take his part. Sometimes I trembled for fear you would agree with me, but you never did. The more I criticised him, the louder you sang his praises, — it was lovely! The fact is, — we might as well throw light upon the whole matter, and then never allude to it again ; and if you do tell Willie Beresford, you shall never visit my manse, nor see me preside at my mothers' meetings, nor hear me address the infant class in the Sunday-school, — the fact is I liked him from the beginning at Lady Baird's dinner. I liked the bow he made when he offered me his arm (I wish it had been his hand) ; I liked the top of his head when it was bowed; I liked his arm when I took it; I liked the height of his shoulder when I stood beside it; I liked the way he put me in my chair (that showed chivalry), and unfolded his napkin (that was neat and businesslike), and pushed aside all his wineglasses but one (that was temperate); I liked the side view of his nose, the shape of his collar, the cleanness of his shave, the manliness of his tone, — oh, I liked him altogether, you must know how it is, Penelope, — the goodness and strength and simplicity that radiated from him. And when he said, within the first half-hour, that international alliances presented even more difficulties to the imagination than others, I felt, to my confusion, a distinct sense of disappointment. Even while I was quarreling with him, I said to myself, 'You poor darling, you cannot have him even if you should want him, so don't look at him much!'— But I did look at him; and what is worse, he looked at me; and what is worse yet, he curled himself so tightly round my heart that if he takes himself away, I shall be cold the rest of my life!"

"Then you are really sure of your love this time, and you have never advised him to wed somebody more worthy than yourself?" I asked.

"Not I!" she replied. "I would n't put such an idea into his head for worlds! He might adopt it!"

XXV

"Pale and wan was she when Glenlogie gaed ben,
But red rosy grew she whene'er he sat doun."
Glenlogie.

JUST here the front door banged, and a manly step sounded on the stair. Francesca sat up straight in a big chair, and dried her eyes hastily with her poor little wet ball of a handkerchief; for she knows that Willie is a privileged visitor in my studio. The door opened (it was ajar), and Ronald Macdonald strode into the room. I hope I may never have the same sense of nothingness again! To be young, pleasing, gifted, and to be regarded no more than a fly upon the wall, is death to one's self-respect.

He dropped on one knee beside Francesca and took her two hands in his without removing his gaze from her speaking face. She burned, but did not flinch under the ordeal. The color leaped into her cheeks. Love swam in her tears, but was not drowned there; it was too strong.

"Did you mean it?" he asked.

She looked at him, trembling, as she said, "I meant every word, and far, far more. I meant all that a girl can say to a man when she loves him, and wants to be everything she is capable of being to him, to his work, to his people, and to his — country."

Even this brief colloquy had been embarrassing, but I knew that worse was still to come and could not be delayed much longer, so I left the room hastily and with no attempt at apology; not that they minded my presence in the least, or observed my exit, though I was obliged to leap over Mr. Macdonald's feet in passing.

I found Mr. Beresford sitting on the stairs, in the lower hall.

"Willie, you angel, you idol, where did you find him?" I exclaimed.

"When I went into the post-office, an hour ago," he replied, "I met Francesca. She asked me for Macdonald's Edinburgh address, saying she had something that belonged to him and wished to send it after him. I offered to address the package and see that it reached him as expeditiously as possible. 'That is what I wish,' she said, with elaborate formality. 'This is something I have just discovered, something he needs very much, something he does not know he has left behind.' I did not think it best to tell her at the moment that Macdonald had not yet deserted Inchcaldy."

"Willie, you have the quickest intelligence and the most exquisite insight of any man I ever met!"

"But the fact was that I had been to see him off, and found him detained by the sudden illness of one of his elders. I rode over again to take him the little parcel. Of course I don't know what it contained; by its size and shape I should judge it might be a thimble, or a collar-button, or a sixpence; but, at all events, he must have needed the thing, for he certainly did not let the grass grow under his feet after he received it! Let us go into the sitting-room until they come down, — as they will have to, poor wretches, sooner or later; I know that I am always being brought down against my will. Salemina wants your advice about the number of her Majesty's portraits to be hung on the front of the cottage, and the number of candles to be placed in each window."

It was a half-hour later when Mr. Macdonald came into the room, and walking directly up to Salemina kissed her hand respectfully.

"Miss Salemina," he said, with evident emotion, "I want to borrow one of your national jewels for my Queen's crown."

"And what will our President say to lose a jewel from his crown?"

"Good republican rulers do not wear coronets, as a matter of principle," he argued; "but in truth I fear I am not thinking of her Majesty — God bless her! This gem is not entirely for state occasions.

'I would wear it in my bosom,
Lest my jewel I should tine.'

It is the crowning of my own life rather than that of the British Empire that engages my present thought. Will you intercede for me with Francesca's father?"

"And this is the end of all your international bickering?" Salemina asked teasingly.

"Yes," he answered; "we have buried the hatchet, signed articles of agreement, made treaties of international comity. Francesca stays over here as a kind of missionary to Scotland, so she says, or as a feminine diplomat; she wishes to be on hand to enforce the Monroe Doctrine properly, in case her government's accredited ambassadors relax in the performance of their duty."

"Salemina!" called a laughing voice outside the door. "I am won'erful lifted up. You will be a prood woman the day, for I am now Estaiblished!" and Francesca, clad in Miss Grieve's Sunday bonnet, shawl, and black cotton gloves, entered and curtsied demurely to the floor. She held, as corroborative detail, a life of John Knox in her hand, and anything more incongruous than her sparkling eyes and mutinous mouth under the melancholy head-gear can hardly be imagined.

"I am now Estaiblished," she repeated. "Div ye ken the new asseestant frae Inchcawdy pairish? I'm the mon" (a second deep curtsy here). "I trust, leddies, that ye 'll mak' the maist o' your releegious preevileges, an' that ye 'll be constant at the kurruk. — Have you given papa's consent, Salemina? And is n't it dreadful that he is Scotch?"

"Is n't it dreadful that she is not?" asked Mr. Macdonald. "Yet to my mind no woman in Scotland is half as lovable as she!"

"And no man in America begins to compare with him," Francesca confessed sadly. "Is n't it pitiful that out of the millions of our own countrypeople we could n't have found somebody that would do? What do you think now, Lord Ronald Macdonald, of those dangerous international alliances?"

"You never understood that speech of mine," he replied, with prompt mendacity. "When I said that international marriages presented more difficulties to the imagination than others, I was thinking of your marriage and mine, and that, I knew from the first moment I saw you, would be extremely difficult to arrange!"

XXVI

> " And soon a score of fires, I ween,
>   From height, and hill, and cliff, were seen;
>   . . . .
>   Each after each they glanced to sight,
>   As stars arise upon the night.
>   They gleamed on many a dusky tarn,
>   Haunted by the lonely earn;
>   On many a cairn's grey pyramid,
>   Where urns of mighty chiefs lie hid."
>   *The Lay of the Last Minstrel.*

THE rain continued at intervals throughout the day, but as the afternoon wore on the skies looked a trifle more hopeful. It would be "saft," no doubt, climbing the Law, but the bonfire must be lighted. Would Pettybaw be behind London? Would Pettybaw desert the Queen in her hour of need? Not though the rain were bursting the well-heads on Cawda; not though the swollen mountain burns drowned us to the knee! So off we started as the short midsummer night descended.

We were to climb the Law, wait for the signal from Cawda's lonely height, and then fire Pettybaw's torch of loyalty to the little lady in black; not a blaze flaming out war and rumors of war, as was the beacon-fire on the old gray battlements of Edinburgh Castle in the days of yore, but a message of peace and good will. Pausing at a hut on the side of the great green mountain, we looked north toward Helva, white-crested with a wreath of vapor. (You need not look on your map of Scotland for Cawda and Helva, for you will not find them any more than you will find Pettybaw and Inchcaldy.) One by one the tops of the distant hills began to clear, and with the glass we could discern the bonfire cairns upbuilt here and there for Scotland's evening sacrifice of love and fealty. Cawda was still veiled, and Cawda was to give the signal for all the smaller fires. Pettybaw's, I suppose, was counted as a flash in the pan, but not one of the hundred patriots climbing the mountain side would have acknowledged it; to us the good name of the kingdom of Fife and the glory of the British Empire depended on Pettybaw fire. Some of us had misgivings, too, — misgivings founded upon Miss Grieve's dismal prophecies. She had agreed to put nine lighted candles in each of our cottage windows at ten o'clock, but had declined to go out of her kitchen to see a procession, hear a band, or look at a bonfire. She had had a sair sickenin' day, an amount of work too wearifu' for one person by her lane. She hoped that the bonfire wasna built o' Mrs. Sinkler's coals nor Mr. Macbrose's kindlings, nor soaked with Mr. Cameron's paraffine; and she finished with the customary but irrelative and exasperating allusion to the exceedingly nice family with whom she had lived in Glasgy.

And still we toiled upward, keeping our doubts to ourselves. Jean was limping bravely, supported by Robin Anstruther's arm. Mr. Macdonald was ardently helping Francesca, who can climb like a chamois, but would doubtless rather be assisted. Her gypsy face shone radiant out of her black cloth hood, and Ronald's was no less luminous. I have never seen two beings more love-daft. They comport themselves as if they had read the manuscript of the tender passion, and were moving in exalted superiority through a less favored world,—a world waiting impatiently for the first number of the story to come out.

Still we climbed, and as we approached the Grey Lady (a curious rock very near the summit) somebody proposed three cheers for the Queen.

How the children hurrahed,—for the infant heart is easily inflamed,—and how their shrill Jubilee slogan pierced the mystery of the night, and went rolling on from glen to glen to the Firth of Forth itself! Then there was a shout from the rocketmen far out on the open moor,— "Cawda's clear! Cawda's clear!" Back against a silver sky stood the signal pile, and signal rockets flashed upward, to be answered from all the surrounding hills.

Now to light our own fire. One of the village

committee solemnly took off his hat and poured on oil. The great moment had come. Brenda Macrae approached the sacred pile, and, tremulous from the effect of much contradictory advice, applied the torch. Silence, thou Grieve and others, false prophets of disaster! Who now could say that Pettybaw bonfire had been badly built, or that its fifteen tons of coal and twenty cords of wood had been unphilosophically heaped together!

The flames rushed toward the sky with ruddy blaze, shining with weird effect against the black fir-trees and the blacker night. Three cheers more! God save the Queen! May she reign over us, happy and glorious! And we cheered lustily, too, you may be sure! It was more for the woman than the monarch; it was for the blameless life, not for the splendid monarchy; but there was everything hearty, and nothing alien in our tone, when we sang "God Save the Queen" with the rest of the Pettybaw villagers.

The land darkened; the wind blew chill. Willie, Mr. Macdonald, and Mr. Anstruther brought rugs, and found a sheltered nook for us where we might still watch the scene. There we sat, looking at the plains below, with all the village streets sparkling with light, with rockets shooting into the air and falling to earth in golden rain, with red lights flickering on the gray lakes, and with one beacon-fire after another gleaming from the hilltops, till we could count more than fifty answering one another from the wooded crests along the shore, some of them piercing the rifts of low-lying clouds till they seemed to be burning in mid-heaven.

Then, one by one, the distant fires faded, and as some of us still sat there silently, far, far away in the gray east there was a faint flush of carmine where the new dawn was kindling in secret. Underneath that violet bank of cloud the sun was forging his beams of light. The pole-star paled. The breath of the new morrow stole up out of the rosy gray. The wings of the morning stirred and trembled; and in the darkness and chill and mysterious awakening, eyes looked into other eyes, hand sought hand, and cheeks touched each other in mute caress.

XXVII

> "Sun, gallop down the westlin skies,
>   Gang soon to bed, an' quickly rise;
> O lash your steeds, post time away,
> And haste about our bridal day!"
> *The Gentle Shepherd.*

EVERY noon, during this last week, as we have wended our way up the loaning to the Pettybaw inn for our luncheon, we have passed three magpies sitting together on the topmost rail of the fence. I am not prepared to state that they were always the same magpies; I only know there were always three of them. We have just discovered what they were about, and great is the excitement in our little circle. I am to be married to-morrow, and married in Pettybaw, and Miss Grieve says that in Scotland the number of magpies one sees is of infinite significance: that one means sorrow; two, mirth; three, a marriage; four, a birth, and we now recall as corroborative detail that we saw one magpie, our first, on the afternoon of her arrival.

Mr. Beresford has been cabled for, and must return to America at once on important business. He persuaded me that the Atlantic is an ower large body of water to roll between two lovers, and I agreed with all my heart.

A wedding was arranged, mostly by telegraph, in six hours. The Reverend Ronald and the Friar are to perform the ceremony; a dear old painter friend of mine, a London R. A., will come to give me away; Francesca will be my maid of honor; Elizabeth Ardmore and Jean Dalziel, my bridemaidens; Robin Anstruther, the best man; while Jamie and Ralph will be kilted pages-in-waiting, and Lady Ardmore will give the breakfast at the castle.

Never was there such generosity, such hospitality, such wealth of friendship! True, I have no wedding finery; but as I am perforce a Scottish bride, I can be married in the white gown with the silver thistles in which I went to Holyrood.

Mr. Anstruther took a night train to and from London, to choose the bouquets and bridal souvenirs. Lady Baird has sent the veil, and a wonderful diamond thistle to pin it on,—a jewel fit for a princess! With the dear Dominie's note promising to be an usher came an antique silver casket filled with white heather. And as for the bride-cake, it is one of Salemina's gifts, chosen as much in a spirit of fun as affection. It is surely appropriate for this American wedding transplanted to Scottish soil, and what should it be but a model, in fairy icing, of Sir Walter's beautiful monument in Princes Street! Of course Francesca is full of nonsensical quips about it, and says that the Edinburgh jail would have been just as fine architecturally (it is, in truth, a building beautiful enough to tempt an æsthete to crime), and a much more fitting symbol for a wedding-cake, — unless, indeed, she adds, Salemina intends her gift to be a monument to my folly.

Pettybaw kirk is trimmed with yellow broom from these dear Scottish banks and braes; and waving their green fans and plumes up and down the aisle where I shall walk a bride, are tall ferns and bracken from Crummylowe Glen, where we played ballads.

As I look back upon it, the life here has been all a ballad from first to last. Like the elfin Tam Lin,

> "The queen o' fairies she caught me
> In this green hill to dwell,"

and these hasty nuptials are a fittingly romantic ending to the summer's poetry. I am in a mood, were it necessary, to be "ta'en by the milk-white hand," lifted to a pillion on a coal-black charger, and spirited "o'er the border an' awa'" by my dear Jock o' Hazledean. Unhappily, all is quite regular and aboveboard; no "lord of Langley dale" contests the prize with the bridegroom, but the marriage is at least unique and unconventional; no one can rob me of that sweet consolation.

So "gallop down the westlin skies," dear Sun,

but, prythee, gallop back to-morrow! "Gang soon to bed," an you will, but rise again betimes! Give me Queen's weather, dear Sun, and shine a benison upon my wedding morn!

[*Exit Penelope into the ballad-land of maiden dreams.*]

www.ingramcontent.com/pod-product-compliance
Lightning Source LLC
Chambersburg PA
CBHW031945230426
43672CB00010B/2052